Sharon Whittaker

PRE-INTERMEDIATE

Total English

DIGITAL
User's Guide

PEARSON
Longman

PROMETHEAN

Contents

Introduction   page 3

Get started   page 6

Unit 1   page 13

Unit 2   page 17

Unit 3   page 21

Unit 4   page 25

Unit 5   page 28

Unit 6   page 31

Unit 7   page 34

Unit 8   page 37

Unit 9   page 40

Unit 10   page 43

Unit 11   page 46

Unit 12   page 49

Film Bank   page 52

Introduction

Total English Digital is the interactive whiteboard software for use with *Total English* course books. We recognise that learning to use interactive whiteboards, like any new piece of technology, can be intimidating, so this guide aims to give you a jargon-free introduction to using interactive whiteboards in your classroom. The software has been designed to use the reliable content taken from the *Total English Students' Book* in an interactive way that increases student motivation and saves you time.

What is an interactive whiteboard, and how does it work with *Total English Digital*?

An interactive whiteboard is a piece of hardware that looks much like a standard whiteboard, but it connects to a computer and a projector in the classroom to make a very powerful tool. When connected, the interactive whiteboard becomes a giant, touch-sensitive version of the computer screen. Instead of using the mouse, you can control your computer through the interactive whiteboard screen just by touching it with a special pen (or, on some types of boards, with your finger). Anything that can be accessed from your computer can be accessed and displayed on the interactive whiteboard, for example Word documents, PowerPoint presentations, photographs, websites or online materials.

Using special software included with the interactive whiteboard, you can also interact with images and text projected on the board: rearranging them, changing their size, colour, etc. This offers a much more interactive experience than using a standard whiteboard or using a data projector alone.

Total English Digital and this guide provide an excellent starting point in building your confidence with the interactive whiteboard and teaching you about the tools you need and how to use them. The *Total English Digital* software follows the same layout with the same contents as the coursebook. This makes it immediately recognisable and quick and easy to switch between using the book and the interactive whiteboard in class.

What are the benefits of interactive whiteboards and *Total English Digital*?

When you use *Total English Digital*, it will help you understand the benefits of interactive whiteboards in the language classroom.

Convenient and time-saving

Total English Digital acts as a 'one-stop-shop' for all of the *Total English* resources. The Students' Book, listening files, tapescripts and videos as well as selected interactive flipcharts (activities specially-prepared for use on an interactive whiteboard using special software called Activstudio) are all easily accessible in one place and displayed on the interactive whiteboard.

Just by touching the interactive whiteboard screen, you can move quickly and easily from an activity in the Students' Book to an audio track, perhaps looking at the tapescript for post-listening work before returning to the Students' Book. This helps you adapt the pace of your lesson according to the needs of the group and saves lots of time. No more cueing CDs or DVDs!

Focuses students' attention

The interactive whiteboard provides a useful focal point in the class. Instead of asking learners to focus on a picture or instruction in the book, you can zoom into the relevant section of the page and magnify it many times on the interactive whiteboard. Just click on any part of the page to make it zoom.

The clear icons and simple controls mean that you and your students can work directly with the interactive whiteboard and avoid going back and forth from the computer to the board. Because you can stay at the front of the classroom, it is easier to keep students' attention focused on the activity at hand.

Engages different types of learners

Some students prefer to listen and absorb, others respond well to pictures, while others respond well to physical interaction. *Total English Digital* supports users with all these preferences through its rich multi-media, audio-visual and flipchart content. The flipcharts involve a range of simple interactions, such as drag and drop, erase or write-in.

The simplicity of these exercise types means that your learners can interact with the materials with no previous typing or IT skills, facilitating more student-centred lessons. Learning becomes more active and, therefore, more memorable.

Helpful and supportive

This guide includes teacher's notes for every flipchart with suggestions on how to teach the lesson using the interactive whiteboard. There are also teaching tips and suggestions on how to exploit the flipcharts and materials further.

By using *Total English Digital*, you'll become familiar with interactive whiteboard technology in general and develop a repertoire of approaches to suit your teaching style. Gradually, *Total English Digital* will give you the confidence to create your own flipchart activities.

Adds variety

Total English Digital is an additional way of presenting *Total English* coursebook material in your lesson. It is not, however, designed to replace the book for the student, nor is it designed to dominate your classroom teaching throughout each lesson. In any classroom situation it is important to select the appropriate tool, approach or materials to best achieve your teaching objectives.

You may, for example, only want to use *Total English Digital* to introduce an activity to be completed in the book or to conduct feedback after a pair or group activity.

How do I teach with *Total English Digital*?

Total English Digital cuts down on preparation time and aims to make teaching with an interactive whiteboard easy. As with any tool, the more familiar you are with it, the easier you will find it and the more confident you will feel in class. In the initial stages, you might prefer to limit your use of the software in class to the 'zoomable' page spreads and the easy-access audio, tapescripts and videos. When you are comfortable with these, you can move on to use the flipcharts.

Familiarise yourself

If you can, look at all the interactive materials available in *Total English Digital*, including the flipchart activities, audio and tapescripts for the module you are about to teach. Not all of the parts of the page have flipcharts but all parts of the book can be magnified to draw students' focus. Think about how and when the interactive whiteboard will make an impact in your lesson. When is it best to use interactive activities, and when is it best for students to work in their books?

Think about how students will be interacting at different stages of the lesson, in whole class, small groups or individual learning mode. At what stages will the learners be actively using the board, and at what stages will it be providing visual support? And don't forget to give your students a break from the digital edition! Sometimes switching the board off/muting the projector can be less distracting and help students focus better on the task in hand, especially with small group and discussion tasks. Remember to think about variety and balance.

Familiarise yourself with the mechanics of each digital activity and check if it requires drag and drop, erase or write-in. A small tool icon in the rubric reminds you which tool to use. Even though you'll be encouraging your students to do the hands-on work at the board, you'll need to provide both language and technical support on occasions.

Before the class, it's a good idea to check the flipchart and see where the answers appear on the page. In the interests of legibility, this will help you direct your students to write their answers in an appropriate place. The step-by-step unit notes in this guide will help you with this.

Manage the classroom

The interactive whiteboard offers great opportunities for student-centred work at the board, but classroom management is crucial. With gap-fill type activities, for example, it can be time-consuming getting different students out to the board for each answer and can slow the pace of your lesson. Resist the temptation to take over the board yourself but rather experiment with ways that work for your group. Depending on the activity type, you might nominate a 'board assistant' for one activity. S/he could elicit answers from the class. Or perhaps use an 'early finisher' or invite individual students to come out while an activity is in progress. In this way the book and interactive whiteboard versions are completed at the same time and the interactive whiteboard provides ongoing feedback.

Reading

With reading activities it is generally more appropriate for students to read the text in their books. The interactive whiteboard provides an excellent focus for pre-reading work and also for post-reading text analysis: highlighting features of the text or vocabulary is a very effective use of the interactive whiteboard.

Writing

If you are preparing students for a writing task, images from the unit make good prompts for brainstorming content and ideas. You might decide to use model texts from the book for process writing activities and can, for example, ask your students to highlight certain features of the text in different colours.

Speaking

In the same way, when planning speaking you may plan to exploit the on-screen tapescripts as model dialogues, highlighting features of spoken discourse in preparation for the main speaking task in the module. You may wish to zoom in on instructions and draw students' attention to key words to make sure they understand what they have to do. You may decide to leave these instructions on screen as they work, or alternatively, zoom in on the *How To …* boxes sections to support the students in their task. As part of general classroom practice, you might drill phrases from these sections, pointing out stress or intonation patterns, so that learners are using a correct model.

Consider if or when you will show the tapescript, and what you will do with it. Decide if there are any useful phrases you want to bring to your students' attention and highlight these with one of the writing tools.

Pronunciation

Pronunciation activities can often be more effective if students are concentrating on imitating the sounds they hear and not trying to read at the same time. This is a good opportunity to ask students to close their books and try to imitate your model or the audio file in *Total English Digital*. You can use the interactive whiteboard to annotate features you want to focus on, for example, stress patterns or phonemic symbols then cover up the patterns so the students practise without reading.

Grammar

In Grammar activities, read through the instructions in the flipchart to see if there are key words you need to explain. You can use the writing tools to highlight these on the board to make sure all your students understand what is expected of them.

Zoom in on the Active grammar boxes or the Reference pages. Use them to teach difficult grammar ideas and give contextualised examples to further support your learners.

Vocabulary

Look at the amount and level of vocabulary coming up in your lesson and decide at what stages of the lesson and how you will introduce it. You can pre-teach phrases by zooming in on pictures from the unit or bringing in other digital images.

Consider how and where you will record new words that come up. You may wish to record them on a blank flipchart or Word document.

Use other resources

You may want to use other traditional or digital resources, for example, a web page, online dictionaries or other teaching materials. Check that any content to be shown on the interactive whiteboard will be visible from the back of the classroom. Try to have digital resources minimised before the lesson so you don't have to search through folders or links during lesson time.

Does the type of interactive whiteboard I'm using make a difference?

No matter what kind of interactive whiteboard you are using, the basic way to use the program is the same.

Promethean interactive whiteboards

If you are using a Promethean interactive whiteboard, *Total English Digital* will launch the 'Professional Edition' of Activstudio software that came with the whiteboard. This version of the software is slightly different from the software described in this guide. You may notice these differences:

- The toolbar is likely to have more tools than the one shown in this guide, but you can use the tools shown in this guide in the same way.
- You are able to have up to five flipcharts open at the same time, including a blank flipchart for note-taking or brainstorming. Any flipchart you create from scratch can be saved.
- You can write/highlight on top of the page spreads when they are zoomed or not zoomed by using 'Annotate-over-desktop' functionality.
- You can use other tools such as a timer, an on-screen keyboard, a link to the internet, etc

Contact your Promethean hardware provider for advice on how to use these additional functions.

Smart, Hitachi Starboard, Ebeam, Polyvision, Mimio or other interactive whiteboards

If you are using a different type of interactive whiteboard, the basic way to use the program remains the same because of the special Activstudio software that is installed as part of *Total English Digital*. By using the software that comes with your interactive whiteboard as well as the tools shown in this guide, you can:

- Write/highlight on top of the page spreads when they are zoomed or not zoomed.
- Have a blank flipchart open for note-taking or brainstorming. These flipcharts can be saved.
- Use other tools such as a timer, an on-screen keyboard, a link to the internet, etc.

Contact your hardware provider for advice on how to use these additional functions.

Support

Pearson Longman wants to help you to feel confident when teaching from *Total English Digital*. If you experience difficulties while using the software, follow these steps until the problem is resolved:

1. Consult the FAQ in this guide (page 11).
2. Restart your computer.
3. Turn the projector and interactive whiteboard off and then on again.
4. Consult the manual that accompanies your interactive whiteboard.
5. If you think it is a problem with your interactive whiteboard, contact the hardware provider.
6. If you think it is a problem with *Total English Digital*, please email the Pearson Longman technical support team at elt-support@pearson.com.

Comments/feedback

Pearson Longman strives to produce high quality products that meet your teaching needs. Please send your comments/ feedback about the product to digitaldelivery@pearson.com.

Get started

Total English Digital home page

Total English Digital is divided into four sections which are accessible through buttons on the home page you see when you install or run the program:

You can move to another section by clicking on the icons:

 Students' Book section to view pages and select interactive whiteboard activities

 Go to Audio Bank

 Go to Film Bank

 Go to Support section

 Return to home page

Audio Bank

Click on any unit.

A list of all the recordings for that unit will appear on the right side of the screen.

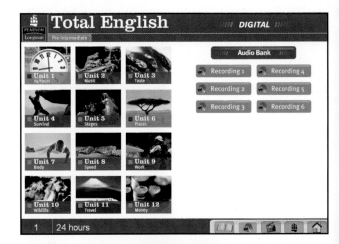

Click on the recording bar [Recording 1] to open the audio player that will play the recording.

You can switch from one section to another using the icons in the bottom navigation bar.

Audio player

Use the slider ●▬▬▬ or the rewind/forward buttons ◄◄ ►► to find a specific part of the audio quickly.
Pressing the Play ► button while the audio is playing will pause the recording. Pressing the button again will play the recording from the point where it was paused.

Use ◄|||||| to control the volume.

Click on 'show' in this panel [AUDIOSCRIPT ▼ SHOW ▮▮ PRINT] to view the tapescript of the recording. Hide the tapescript by clicking on the appropriate button. You can print it with or without annotations.

[_ 🗗 ✕] Click here to minimise, maximise or close the audio player window.

Tapescript window

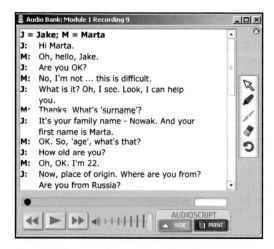

Control the audio using the audio player buttons. Use the small toolbar to control or annotate the tapescript.

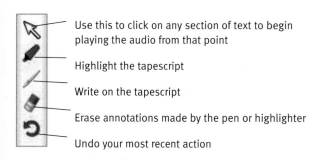

Use this to click on any section of text to begin playing the audio from that point

Highlight the tapescript

Write on the tapescript

Erase annotations made by the pen or highlighter

Undo your most recent action

_|&|X| Click here to minimise, maximise or close the tapescript window.

Film Bank

In the Film Bank select the unit you are studying.
Click on [Watch the film] to open the Film Bank player.

You can switch from one section to another using the icons in the bottom navigation bar.

Film Bank player

Use the slider •━━━━━━ or the rewind/forward buttons ◄◄ ►► to find a specific part of the video quickly. Pressing the Play ► button while the video is playing will pause the video. Pressing the button again will play the video from the point where it was paused.

Click subtitles on to turn on the subtitles.
Click subtitles off to turn off the subtitles.

Use ◄»••┼┼┼┼┼┼┼ to control the volume.

Click [AUDIOSCRIPT ▼SHOW 🖨PRINT] to view the video tapescript. Hide or print it by clicking on the appropriate button. You can print the video tapescript with or without annotations. You can also view the English subtitles by clicking on the 'Subtitles on/off' button on this panel.

Film Bank tapescript

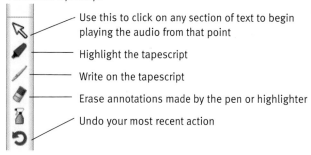

Use this to click on any section of text to begin playing the audio from that point

Highlight the tapescript

Write on the tapescript

Erase annotations made by the pen or highlighter

Undo your most recent action

Click on [▲ HIDE] to hide the tapescript and return the window to its previous size.

Click here to minimise, maximise or close the Film Bank player
_|&|X| window.

Students' Book

Click on any unit to open it.

Small pictures of all the double spreads for that unit will appear:

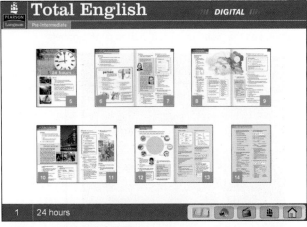

Click on any spread to select it.

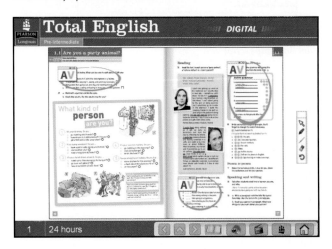

The bottom navigation bar changes to:

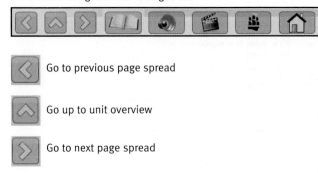

Go to previous page spread

Go up to unit overview

Go to next page spread

Click on any section of the Students' Book page (instructions, pictures, exercises) and it will zoom up to be extra large and easily visible. Click on it again to zoom back out.

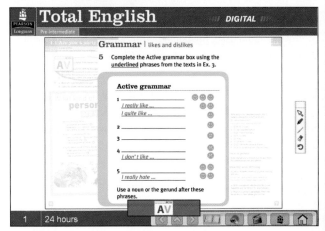

Use the small toolbar to annotate the page spreads or any zoomed-up area

Your annotations will not be saved when you zoom out or change pages.

If a section of the Students' Book is circled, this shows you that there is an either an audio file or an interactive activity for that section. The icon will tell you which one it is: AV, ▣ or ▣ for flipcharts and ▣ for an audio file. Zoom up that section and click on the icon.

The audio recording will behave exactly as it does in the Audio Bank (see page 6).

The flipchart will open in a new window.

What is a flipchart?

Each level of *Total English Digital* includes hundreds of activities specially created to help your students interact directly with the content from the book using interactive whiteboard tools. These interactive activities are called flipcharts. Open a flipchart by clicking on the AV, ☆ ☐ on a zoomed-up part of the page.

AV flipcharts can be used to complete an exercise from the Students' Book using interactive whiteboard tools.

☆ flipcharts contain content *additional* to that in the Students' Book. They encourage further class participation, and have very communicative content.

☐ are Your Ideas flipcharts. These are spaces for brainstorming and class discussion. Notes can easily be made here using / tool.

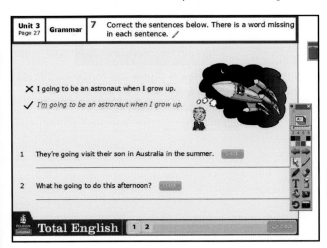

The *Total English Digital* package contains a special type of software called Activstudio (created by one of the leading interactive whiteboard manufacturers, Promethean) that opens a toolbar you can use with the flipcharts no matter what type of interactive whiteboard you have.

The Activstudio toolbar

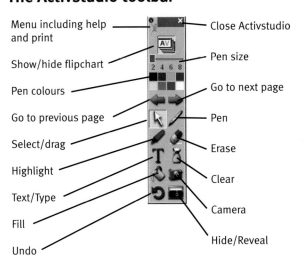

Menu including help and print
Close Activstudio
Show/hide flipchart
Pen size
Pen colours
Go to next page
Go to previous page
Pen
Select/drag
Erase
Highlight
Clear
Text/Type
Camera
Fill
Hide/Reveal
Undo

Other flipchart icons

2.1	Tapescript reference
1 **2**	Go to page 1, 2 etc.
T	Show tapescript/audio player
⦿	Play audio
✓ CHECK	Show answers
⟳	Reset flipchart
🗑	Rubbish bin (drag any annotations onto this icon to delete them from the flipchart)

The main flipchart activity types

1. / Writing

2. ◆ Erasing

3. ✐ Highlighting

4. ⬚ Drag and drop

The main tools needed for each activity type are shown in the rubric area of the page. Clicking on the icons there or in the toolbar will activate that function, causing the interactive whiteboard pen (or your finger) to act as the selected tool, for example, an eraser or a highlighter.

Within each activity type there are variations on how the tools may be used.

1. ✏ Writing

The flipcharts may require you to use the pen in various ways:
– to write words, phrases or sentences;
– to choose an answer by circling or underlying items;
– to draw lines to match halves of sentences.

2 4 6 8 Use the slider to make the pen width thicker.

Use the colour squares to choose a different colour for the 'ink'.

2. 🧽 Erasing

Activities that include the eraser will ask you to erase the wrong answer (and leave the correct answer) or to erase a box to reveal the answer.

3. ✏ Highlighting

Highlighting is used in flipchart activities to show stress during pronunciation practice or to emphasize key points.

4. 🔖 Drag and drop

The arrow tool is used in activities to drag words into the correct category to match words or to move the answer into the gap. It is also used to drag a special 'answer box' down the page to reveal the correct answer.

Support section

The support section includes an on-screen user's guide and quick links to further information and support.

Select the unit for the guide you need or one of the general sections on the right. The guide will open in Adobe Acrobat Reader. If you do not have this installed on your computer already, it is free to download from http://www.adobe.com/downloads/.

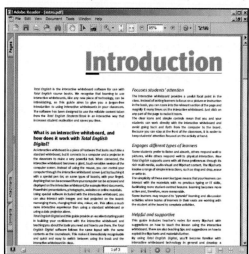

In the support section there is also a link to the *Total English* website where information and material are available.
http:///www.pearsonlongman.com/totalenglish/

FAQ Frequently asked questions

How do I install the software?

When you first insert the CD-ROM into your computer's CD drive, the program will begin to run automatically. It will ask if you want to install or run from CD. Even if you choose to run it directly from the CD-ROM (and are using an interactive whiteboard that is not Promethean brand), you are still required to install Activstudio before *Total English Digital* will work correctly. If you choose to install *Total English Digital*, the program will guide you through the installation.

How do I access Total English Digital?

Go to Start\Programs\Longman and choose your *Total English* level, or click on the desktop icon for the level you want to use.

Is Total English Digital different in any way to the paper edition?

Yes and No. The Students' Book pages contain exactly the same content as the paper edition, so that what your students see on the page is the same as on the screen. In addition, there are direct links to the tapescripts and flipchart activities as well as the Film Bank section. The Film Bank activities, Writing Bank, etc., however, are not included.

How do I access the videos?

You can access the videos directly from the home page when you open the program.

How do I access the Teacher's Book?

A digital copy of the traditional teacher's book is not included; however, unit-by-unit teacher's notes and answer keys for the flipcharts activities are included in this guide.

How do I zoom in/out on a section of the page?

Click on any section of the Students' Book pages, instructions, pictures or exercises, and it will zoom in on the section. Click again to zoom back out.

How do I move forwards and backwards in the Student's Book?

Use ▷ to move to the next page and ◁ to move back a page. If you want to move to another unit, then use ⌂ to go back to the overall view of the unit. Click ⌊⌊⌋ to see the list of units.

What do the circles on the page spreads mean?

They show you that there is an interactive activity with this section of the book; either an audio file or a flipchart activity.

How do I write on a Students' Book page?

You can write on a zoomed or unzoomed part of the Students' Book page using the small tools in the toolbar. Alternatively you can use the software that came with your board. For Promethean board users, this would be Activstudio Professional Edition's 'Annotate-over-desktop' functionality. Other board users should consult their hardware manufacturer for advice on how to access similar functionality.

How do my students have access to the Total English Digital from home?

They don't, the digital edition is only licensed to schools and organisations. The software is not designed for students to self-access. A teacher should facilitate the material for them in a classroom environment.

How can I access Total English Digital from home?

Your licence permits you to install *Total English Digital* on teachers' home computers or laptops so they can access the material to prepare their lessons outside the classroom. The software can be controlled from a computer without the interactive whiteboard being plugged in, but some functions, like writing, are considerably more difficult when using a mouse instead of a pen (or finger)!

How do I access the audio file directly without going through the Students' Book pages?

Go to 🔘 on the home page and choose the audio file from the unit menu.

Do I still need to use a CD for listening activities?

Most activities include the audio, but, for copyright reasons, you will need to use a CD for any songs in the Students' Book. All listening activities from the Workbook must be played from the CD.

How do I see the tapescript?

Click on ▥ in a flipchart to show the tapescript. If this option does not appear, it is because the tapescript is written out on the page of the flipchart.

In the Audio Bank, click ▥ to make the tapescript and its tools appear. If this option doesn't appear, then there is no tapescript included with this audio file because the tapescript is written out as part of the Students' Book.

How do I cue the audio or video tapescript?

Make sure you have selected ⌀ from the small tapescript toolbar. Then, click on a section of the tapescript (it will change colour) to begin playing from this point. You can use also use the normal pause, fast forward/rewind buttons.

How do I write on a tapescript?

Use the mini toolbar next to the tapescript. Click on ✏ to write, ✒ to highlight, 🖊 to erase and ↺ to undo any writing.

How do I make a tapescript bigger?

You can resize the window by dragging a corner or use ▬🗗✕ to minimise, maximise or close it.

How do I print a tapescript?

Click the small picture of the printer on the tapescript toolbar.

Where are the flipcharts?

You can see the AV icon on the double spread or enlarged section of your Students' Book. Click on it to launch the flipchart activity.

How do I check the answers to activities?

Select ▭. Sometimes you can check one by one, or sometimes the whole page at once.

How do I get rid of the flipchart answers?

If showing answers is the last thing you have done, click on ↺ to undo your last step. Otherwise close the flipchart and reopen it to reset the page.

How do I know where the answers are going to appear on the page?

Before you use the page with your students, click on ▭ to see where the answer boxes appear or consult the unit-by-unit notes in this guide. Then make sure you or your students don't write in that area.

How do I write on a flipchart?

Use ✏ from the Activstudio tool bar or click on the ✏ next to the activity instructions.

How do I erase what I've written?

For individual words or small sections, use the 🖊 from the Activstudio tool bar.

How do I reset the page to its original state?

Close the flipchart and reopen it to reset the page.

How do I switch between the flipchart and the Students' Book?

Click on AV at the top of your Activstudio toolbar to temporarily hide the flipchart and take you back to the Student's Book. Click on AV again to bring back your flipchart.

How do I edit or save changes to flipcharts? Can I add my own pictures or text?

You can save any changes you make in a flipchart. Click on the orange figure on the Activstudio toolbar and select 'Flipchart' then 'Save As'. You will need to select a place on your computer to save it. Your saved version will not be opened through the page spreads. You will need to open it from where you saved it.

If you want to create your own flipchart to add pictures or text, you can use your board's own software or choose Flipchart/New from the menu under the orange figure on the Activstudio toolbar.

How do I keep a blank flipchart page open for my own notes?

If you are using the edition of Activstudio that came with *Total English Digital*, you can only have one flipchart open at a time, but you could always switch between a blank page of a Word document or a flipchart in your interactive whiteboard's native software.

If you are using Activstudio Professional Edition then you can have your own flipcharts open at the same time as a *Total English Digital* flipchart. Click on A 'Arrange windows' icon in the top right of your screen to switch between the two flipcharts.

How do I close a flipchart?

Close the Activstudio software by clicking on the cross ▬🗗✕ on the toolbar.

The program will ask you if you want to save your changes. You may save over the original version of the flipchart or save a changed version elsewhere on your computer.

Click on **page 5**. It will expand to fill the screen. Remember, you can zoom in to any part of the page by clicking on it, and return by clicking on it again.

Page 5

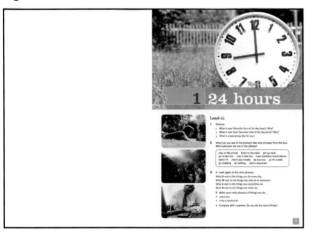

Flipchart: *Your ideas* **p5**

Open the flipchart by clicking on the circled area and then on the Your Ideas button 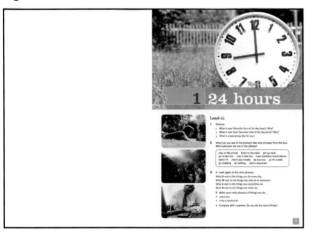.

Use this page to collate ideas from your students. Split the class in half. Ask one side of the room to pair up and discuss their favourite time of day, and ask the other half to talk about their favourite time of the week. Use the pen tool to make notes on their answers. Then repeat the exercise with least favourite.
Close the flipchart by clicking X in the toolbar.
Return to the double spread by clicking on the zoomed-up area to make it smaller.

Flipchart: *Lead-In* **p5**

Open the flipchart by clicking on the circled area and then on the flipchart button AV.

3a Because of the length, this exercise is on two pages 1 and
2.

Focus the students' attention on the verb phrases on the interactive whiteboard and give some examples about yourself e.g., *I chat on the phone every day.* Now tell the students to work individually, writing an appropriate letter next to each activity in their books.
Click on the arrow button in the toolbar or in the rubric and ask a student to come to the interactive whiteboard to click on the letters and drag them down next to the appropriate verb phrase for them. (There are multiple copies of each letter).
Click on 2 at the bottom to move to the next page for the last part of the exercise and continue.
See if there is any general agreement with the rest of the class. Ask the student to click on the Highlighter button in the toolbar and highlight any activities where the whole class agree.
Choose a different colour by clicking on one of the coloured squares in the toolbar and highlight activities that the class like.

> **TIP:** *If students make a mistake, click on the Undo button* ↺ *in the toolbar to delete the last stroke.*

b Click on 3 . Give the students a few minutes in pairs to

brainstorm other verb phrases that fit the two categories.
Click on the pen button in the toolbar or rubric and ask for volunteers to come to the interactive whiteboard to write some of their suggestions in the two columns.

> **TIP:** *Use the slider control in the toolbar to change the width of the pen. Change the pen colour by clicking on one of the small coloured squares below the slider.*

Tell the students to copy down any new expressions, with an appropriate letter alongside (D, W, S or N).
c Click on the next page arrow ➡ in the toolbar to go to the next page, which is empty, and write an example exchange on the board e.g., *I stay in bed late at weekends. What about you?*
Remind students that *always/never* go before the main verb and *every day/at the weekend* go at the end of the sentence. Students compare their lists with a partner (preferably a different one than before) to see what they have in common.
Close the flipchart by clicking X in the toolbar.
Return to the double spread by clicking on the zoomed-up area to make it smaller.
Click on ▶ to go to the next double spread.

Double Spread p6/7

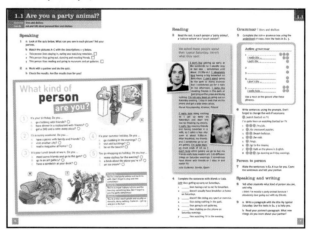

Flipchart: *Speaking* **p6**

Open the flipchart by clicking on the circled area and then on AV.
1a Focus students' attention on the pictures on the interactive whiteboard. They discuss with a partner what they can see in each picture. Encourage them to be as detailed as possible. Point to each picture in turn on the interactive whiteboard and get feedback from a number of students.

> **TIP:** *Click on* ✎ *and write any relevant vocabulary below or above the corresponding picture.*

b Click on 2 . In pairs, students match the descriptions and the pictures in their books.
Click on in the toolbar or in the rubric and ask a student to come to the interactive whiteboard, click on the pictures on the left one by one and drag them up and down until they correspond with the sentences. Ask the student to read the sentence aloud and point to the corresponding picture.

Click on the check button ◻ at the bottom to check and display the letter in boxes below each sentence.

> **ANSWERS**
> 1 picture B   2 picture C   3 picture A

Close the flipchart by clicking X in the toolbar.
Return to the double spread by clicking on the zoomed-up area to make it smaller.

Flipchart: *Reading* **p7**
Open the flipchart by clicking on the circled area and then on ◻.
4 Because of the length, this exercise is on two pages ◻ and ◻ .
Students complete the sentences in their books in pairs.
Click on ◻ and ask a student to come to the interactive whiteboard to complete a sentence by choosing one of the names, Lola or Marek, from the top and dragging it onto the appropriate line. Ask the student to read out the completed sentence and ask if the whole group agree. Discuss as necessary.
Click on ◻ to display the answers in boxes below the lines.
Click on ◻ and complete the exercise in the same way.
Alternatively, you can click on ◻ and finish the exercise and then return to ◻ to click on ◻ and check each page in turn.

> **ANSWERS**
> 1 Marek 2 Lola 3 Marek 4 Marek 5 Lola 6 Marek 7 Lola

Close the flipchart by clicking X in the toolbar.
Return to the double spread by clicking on the zoomed-up area to make it smaller.

Flipchart: *Grammar* **p7**
Open the flipchart by clicking on the circled area and then on ◻.
5 Focus students' attention on the Active grammar box on the interactive whiteboard and establish the fact that the faces represent different degrees of liking and not liking. Tell the students to work with a partner to complete the gaps in their books by looking back at the expressions underlined in the Reading text. Click on ◻ and ask a student to come to the interactive whiteboard to complete the Active grammar box by dragging the missing phrases from the right onto the lines in the correct place in the Active grammar box.

Click on ◻ to display the answers on a new page.
Click on ◻ at the bottom to return to ◻ to compare your answers.

> **ANSWERS**
> I absolutely love 2 I'm quite keen on 3 I don't mind
> 4 I'm not very keen on 5 I can't stand

> **TIP:** *For additional practice, click on the reset button ◻ in the toolbar to return to the original ◻ and then cover the Active grammar box on the left by clicking on the reveal button ◻ in the toolbar, and then clicking on the right hand part of the cover and dragging it to the left to show only the list of phrases. Click on ◻ and ask a student to come to the interactive whiteboard to drag the phrases into the correct order as they appear in the Active grammar box. Click on the cover and drag it to the left to check. Click on ◻ to remove the cover.*

Click on ◻ to show the answer page again, click on ◻ and draw students' attention to the note at the bottom of the grammar box by highlighting it. Click on ◻ and write the following examples from the text on the board. *Noun: modern art. Gerund: getting up early.* Ask students to find more examples of the gerund in the text (*having, going, doing, meeting, lying, checking*) and discuss with a partner the rules we use to make this form. Ask a student to come to the interactive whiteboard to complete a sentence with something that is true for them. Ask that student to nominate another student to come up and continue and so on.
Close the flipchart by clicking X in the toolbar.
Return to the double spread by clicking on the zoomed-up area to make it smaller.
Click on ◻ to go to the next double spread.

Double Spread p8/9

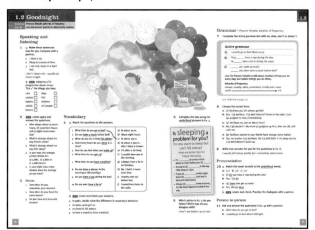

Flipchart: *Speaking and Listening* **p8**
Open the flipchart by clicking on the circled area and then on ◻.
b Tell the students they are going to listen to a TV programme about sleep habits. Focus their attention on the list of items on the interactive whiteboard that might be mentioned and read through them with the whole class. Click on the audio button ◻ at the bottom to play recording 1.1 Then, in their books, students tick the items they hear.

> **TIP:** *You can move the audio window to a different place on the screen by clicking on its title bar and dragging the window to the desired location, where it is not covering text.*

Click on ◻ and ask a student to come to the interactive whiteboard to put a tick next to the things they heard.
Click on ◻ to display the answers next to the boxes.

> **ANSWERS**
> cats, horses, fish, babies, children, adults

2 Click on ◻ . This exercise is on two pages, ◻ and ◻ . Tell the students to read through the questions in their books with a partner and suggest answers for each one based on what they can remember from the recording. Click on ◻ to play recording 1.1 again and students answer the questions in their books. Tell them to check their answers with a partner. Click on ◻ in the toolbox or in the rubric and ask a student to come to the interactive whiteboard and write along the lines to answer the questions. You can either click on ◻ at the end of each question and check answers as you go along, or click on ◻ at the bottom and

check all answers for that page together. Similarly, you can either check page 2 as soon as you finish it and then move to 3 , or click on 3 and finish the whole exercise before returning to 2 to check.

Click on ▨▨▨ to display the answers in boxes below the lines.

> **ANSWERS**
> 1a fish 1b (newborn) babies 1c adults   2 They sleep standing up.   3 They don't close their eyes. 4 2,688
> 5 four or five

Close the flipchart by clicking X in the toolbar.
Return to the double spread by clicking on the zoomed-up area to make it smaller.

Flipchart: *Vocabulary* p8

Open the flipchart by clicking on the circled area and then on ᴀᵛ .
4a Students work in pairs to match the questions and answers in their books.
Click on ⌇ and ask a student to come to the interactive whiteboard and drag the answers in the right-hand column up and down until they correspond to the correct question.

> **TIP:** *Drag temporarily unwanted answers out of the way and 'park' them on top of the lines to avoid overwriting.*

Click on ▨▨▨ to display the answers on a new page.
Click on ▨ to return to 1 to compare your answers.

> **ANSWERS**
> 1 c) 2 i) 3 j) 4 b) 5 e) 6 a) 7 d) 8 f) 9 h) 10 g)

> **TIP:** *Click on ◉ to play recording 1.2 and students check/confirm their answers.*

Close the flipchart by clicking X in the toolbar.
Return to the double spread by clicking on the zoomed-up area to make it smaller.
Click on ▧ to go to the next double spread.

Flipchart: *Your ideas* p9

Open the flipchart by clicking on the circled area and then on the Your Ideas button ᴺ▯
Using the picture as a prompt, talk about how to fall asleep quicker. Make notes using the pen tool and remember you can print off the notes directly from the interactive whiteboard.
Close the flipchart by clicking X in the toolbar.
Return to the double spread by clicking on the zoomed-up area to make it smaller.
Click on ▧ to go to the next double spread.

Double Spread p10/11

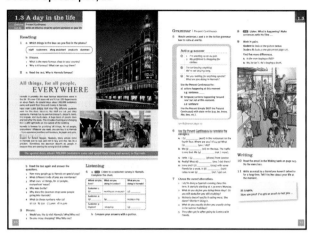

Flipchart: *Listening* p10

Open the flipchart by clicking on the circled area and then on ᴀᵛ .
4a Click on ✎ and highlight *customer survey* on the board. Ask the students if they know what this is. Elicit or explain that it's a kind of questionnaire, which is normally used in market research. Ask the students if they can imagine what type of questions would be included in this type of survey. Get various suggestions from the class. Highlight the three chart headings and tell the students that they have to complete the gaps in their books. Click on ◉ at the bottom to play recording 1.4.

> **TIP:** *Drag the audio window down to the bottom away from the chart.*

b After listening to the recording, students compare with a partner. Play the recording again if you feel it is necessary. Click on ✎ and ask a student to come to the interactive whiteboard to write on the lines to complete the chart.
You can either click on ▨▨▨ at the ends of each row to check answers as you go along, or finish the chart and then click on ▨▨▨ at the bottom to check all the answers together.

Clicking on ▨▨▨ will display the answers in boxes below the lines.

> **ANSWERS**
> 1 Spain 2 just looking 3 Poland 4 on holiday 5 shopping (for clothes) for a wedding

Close the flipchart by clicking X in the toolbar.
Return to the double spread by clicking on the zoomed-up area to make it smaller.

Flipchart: *Grammar* p11

Open the flipchart by clicking on the circled area and then on ᴀᵛ .
Students choose the correct alternative in their books with a partner. Click on ✐ in the toolbar or in the rubric and ask a student to come to the interactive whiteboard and erase the wrong alternative.

> **TIP:** *If students make a mistake, click on ⟲ in the toolbar to delete the last stroke. You can also change the width of the eraser with the slider, in the same way as with the pen.*

Click on [image] to highlight the correct alternatives.
You can either check each sentence as you work through by clicking on the small individual [image]s at the end of each line or check all the sentences together at the end by clicking on the larger [image] at the bottom.

> **ANSWERS**
> 1 'm doing/starts 2 are you doing/Are you still studying 3 doesn't eat/doesn't like 4 do you usually do 5 often go

Close the flipchart by clicking X in the toolbar.
Return to the double spread by clicking on the zoomed-up area to make it smaller.
Click on [image] to go to the next double spread.

Double Spread p12/13

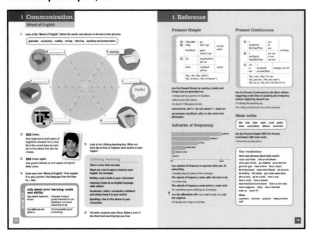

Flipchart: *Communication* **p12**
Open the flipchart by clicking on the circled area and then on [AV].
1 Students work in pairs to write the words on the correct part of the wheel in their books. Click on [image] and ask a student to come to the interactive whiteboard and drag the words from the column on the right to the correct box on the 'Wheel of English'.

Click on [image] to display the answers on a new page.
Click on [image] to return to [1] to compare your answers.

> **ANSWERS**
> A listening (4) B grammar (3) C speaking and pronunciation (5) D writing (2) E vocabulary (4) F reading (3)

Click on [2].
Listen to recording 1.6.
Ask a student to come to the board and write feedback from the class on the wheel.
Use the [pen] tool.
Click on [image] to see the correct answers.
Close flipchart by clicking X in the toolbar.
Return to the double spread by clicking on the zoomed-up area to make it smaller.

Flipchart: *Special flipchart* **p12**
Open the flipchart by clicking on the circled area and then on the Special Flipchart button [image]
Ask students to look at the wheel in their books and, working in pairs, decide what their priorities are when it comes to learning English. Ask them to make some brief notes (if they need to) and then explain their reasons. Ask volunteers to come to the interactive whiteboard and, using the pen tool [pen], demonstrate their answers.
Close the flipchart by clicking X in the toolbar.
Return to the double spread by clicking on the zoomed-up area to make it smaller.
Click on the upwards pointing arrow [image] to return to Unit 1, and then [image] to return to the contents page to go to the next module.

Click on **page 15**. It will expand to fill the screen. Remember, you can zoom in to any part of the page by clicking on it, and return by clicking on it again.

Page 15

Flipchart: *Your ideas* **p15**
Open the flipchart by clicking on the circled area and then on the Your Ideas button ⬚.
Ask the students to make suggestions about the kinds of musical instruments that they can play. They can write or draw on the board with the ✏ tool and you can print out their ideas.
Close the flipchart by clicking X in the toolbar.
Return to the double spread by clicking on the zoomed-up area to make it smaller.

Flipchart: *Lead-in* **p15**
Open the flipchart by clicking on the circled area and then on the flipchart button ⬚.

3a Because of its length, this exercise is on two pages ▣ and ▣ .
Focus on the words and phrases in the box at the top and check that students understand all of them. Explain any they don't.
Students complete the sentences in their books with the correct expression and check in pairs.
Click on ⬚ and ask a student to come to the interactive whiteboard to drag the vocabulary from the box at the top onto the lines to complete the sentences.
You can either check each sentence as you work through by clicking on the small individual ⬚s at the end of each sentence or check all the sentences together at the end by clicking on the larger ⬚ at the bottom. Similarly, you can click on ▣ and finish the whole exercise before checking; or check ▣ before moving on to do ▣ .

Clicking on ⬚ will display the answers in boxes below the lines.

> **ANSWERS**
> 1 favourite band 2 last concert 3 download 4 read music
> 5 compilation CDs 6 favourite record 7 lead singer
> 8 really into

> **TIP:** *Click on the reset button ↻ in the toolbar. Click on ⬚ and drag the cover down to reveal only the vocabulary in the box. Ask students to choose one of the words or phrases and try to remember the example sentence from the practice. As they choose, click on ✏ and highlight the choices. Click on ⬚ again to remove the cover.*

Close the flipchart by clicking X in the toolbar.
Return to the double spread by clicking on the zoomed-up area to make it smaller.
Click on ⟩⟩ to go to the next double spread.

Double Spread p16/17

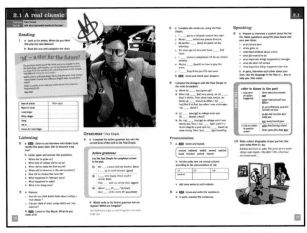

Flipchart: *Grammar* **p16**
Open the flipchart.
4a Focus students' attention on the Active grammar box and have them complete the gaps in their books with a partner.
Click on ✏ and ask a student to come to the interactive whiteboard to write the correct form of the verb on the line.

> **TIP:** *Click on ↺ in the toolbar if students make a mistake. This will erase the last pen stroke.*

Click on ⬚ to display the answers on a new page.
Click on ⬚ to return to ▣ to compare your answers.

> **ANSWERS**
> + We formed a band with my brother. I grew up in South London.
> – I did not (didn't) feel very happy about my first record. They did not (didn't) agree with me all the time.
> ? Where did it all start? How did you think of the name M?

Explain they can use the complete form *did not* or the contracted form *didn't*, (more common in spoken English). Explain: We use this tense to refer to finished actions in the past.

> **TIP:** *Use ✏ to highlight relevant language. Click on the coloured squares in the toolbar to change the colour.*

b Click on [2] . Students discuss the question in pairs and mark the regular verbs in their books. Refer students to the Reference page 23 and the irregular verb table on page 149.

Click on ✏ and ask a student to come to the interactive whiteboard to write the verbs in the correct column.

> **TIP:** *Use a different colour for regular and irregular verbs by clicking on one of the coloured squares in the toolbar.*

Click on ▨ to display the answers in boxes below the columns.

> **ANSWERS**
> Regular verbs: form, agree, start
> Irregular verbs: grow, feel, think

Close the flipchart.

Flipchart: *Pronunciation* **p17**
Open the flipchart.
Click on ◉ at the bottom to play recording 2.5 and students repeat each word.

> **TIP:** *There is a pause after each word to give students time to repeat, but if you need more time it is easy to just click on the slider, hold to pause and then release to continue. Remember you can drag the audio window to a more convenient position.*

b In pairs, students put the verbs into the correct column in their books. Encourage them to pronounce the words together as they do this and discuss the pronunciation rules.

Click on ↖ in the toolbar or in the rubric and ask a student to come to the interactive whiteboard to drag the verbs into the correct column depending on the pronunciation.

Click on ▨ to display the answers (and explanations) in boxes below the columns.

> **ANSWERS**
> \t\ worked, finished, kissed (if the verb ends in an unvoiced consonant) \d\ believed, moved, loved (if the verb ends in a voiced sound)
> \id\ ended, wanted, waited (if the verb ends in -d or -t)

> **TIP:** *Click on ✏ to use the highlighter to colour the endings to make them memorable for students. Ask the students which colours they would like.*

c Students work in pairs to think of more verbs for each list. Click on ✏ and ask a student to come to the interactive whiteboard to write any suggested verbs in the appropriate column.

> **TIP:** *Use corresponding pen colours for each column.*

> **SUGGESTED ANSWERS**
> \t\ passed, walked \d\ seemed, played \id\ painted, visited

Close the flipchart.
Click on ▨ to go to the next double spread.

Double Spread p18/19

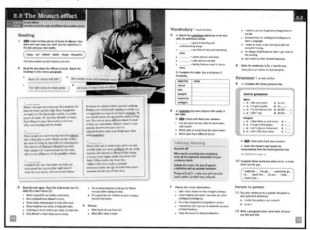

Flipchart: *Reading* **p18**
Open the flipchart.
3 Ask various students to read the statements aloud from the interactive whiteboard and check that everybody understands. Students read the text in their books again and decide if those statements were true or false or if the text doesn't say (don't know). Students check with a partner.

Click on ✏ in the toolbar or in the rubric and ask a student to come to the interactive whiteboard to put a tick, cross or DK in the box at the end of each line.

You can either check each sentence as you work through by clicking on the small individual ▨ s at the end of each line or check all the sentences together at the end by clicking on the larger ▨ at the bottom.

Clicking on ▨ will display the answers after the boxes.

> **ANSWERS**
> 1 T 2 DK 3 T 4 DK 5 F 6 F 7 DK 8 T

> **TIP:** *Involve the students in a vocabulary review exercise. Click on ✏ , use the slider on the toolbar to make the pen width thicker, and ask a student to come and blank out some words in the sentences to test the others. Click on ♠ and students have to write down the missing words. Then slowly rub out the colour to reveal the word and students can check. This could also be done as a team game.*

Close the flipchart.

Flipchart: *Your ideas* **p18**
Open the flipchart by clicking on the circled area and then on the Your Ideas button ▥
Ask students to think about their favourite songs or pieces of music. Make notes on their suggestions, using different coloured ✏ tools.
Close the flipchart by clicking X in the toolbar.
Return to the double spread by clicking on the zoomed-up area to make it smaller.

Flipchart: *Vocabulary* **p19**
Open the flipchart.
7 Because of the length, this exercise is on two pages [1] and [2].
Students work in pairs to choose the correct alternative in their

books. Click on ✎ and ask a student to come to the interactive whiteboard to erase the incorrect alternative.

> **TIP:** *If students make a mistake, click on ↻ to delete the last stroke. Also you can change the width of the eraser if necessary by using the slider bar in the toolbar.*

You can either click on [▭] at the ends of each line to check answers consecutively, or click on [▭] at the bottom to check all the answers together.
Similarly, you can click on [2] and finish the exercise and then return to [1] to check each page, or check at the end of [1] before going on to [2].
Clicking on [▭] will highlight the answers.

> **ANSWERS**
> 1 energetic 2 intelligent 3 imaginative 4 tiredness
> 5 relaxation 6 imagination 7 intelligence 8 energy 9 tired
> 10 relaxed

> **TIP:** *Click on ✐ to highlight different parts of speech (adjectives and nouns) with different colours.*

> **TIP:** *For vocabulary review, now or later, use ✎ to erase all the words. Click on ✐ and ask students to see if they can write the word under the sentence. Then click on [▭] to check as before.*

Close the flipchart.
Click on [▷] to go to the next double spread.

Double Spread p20/21

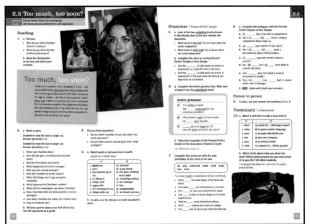

Flipchart: *Reading* p20
Open the flipchart.
4a In their books, students match phrases from column A with phrases from column B.
Click on ⬐ and ask a student to come to the interactive whiteboard and drag the words in column B up and down until they correspond with the correct combination.

Click on [▭] to display the answers on the right.

> **ANSWERS**
> 1 g) 2 d) 3 a) 4 h) 5 b) 6 e) 7 c) 8 f)

> **TIP:** *Use the phrases as prompts to help students to tell the story again, filling in any extra information they can remember. Click on ▭ in the toolbar to cover the screen and click in the top quarter and drag the cover down to reveal the first phrase. Click on ✐ and make any changes to the form of the words to fit in with the story. Drag the cover down to reveal the next phrase and continue in this way. Depending on your students, you can either reveal the prompt first or see if they can remember and then reveal it.*

Close the flipchart.

Flipchart: *Grammar* p21
Open the flipchart.
7 Students work in pairs to complete the sentences in their books.
Click on ⬐ and ask a student to come to the interactive whiteboard to write in the correct version of the verbs in the box.
You can either click on [▭] at the ends of each line to check answers as you go through, or click on [▭] at the bottom to check all the answers together.

Clicking on [▭] will display the answers in boxes below the lines.

> **ANSWERS**
> 1 met 2 played 3 been 4 worked 5 bought 6 studied
> 7 downloaded

> **TIP:** *Use this exercise as a review later. Click on ▭, click at the bottom and drag the cover up to reveal all the sentences. Click on ✐ and see if students can remember the missing verbs and their correct past participles and write them in.*

Close the flipchart.

Flipchart: *Grammar* p21
Open the flipchart.
8a Because of the length, this exercise is on two pages [1] and [2].
Students work in pairs to complete the dialogues in their books.
Click on ✐ and ask a student to come to the interactive whiteboard to write the correct form of the verb along the lines.
Click on [▭] to display the answers above the lines.
You can either click on [▭] at the ends of each line to check answers as you go through, or click on [▭] at the bottom to check all the answers together.
Alternatively, you can click on [2] and finish the exercise and then return to [1] to check each page.
Discuss reasons for mistaken tenses.
You may also choose to wait and check your answers from the audio.

> **ANSWERS**
> 1 Have you ever won 2 have 3 won 4 Did you watch 5 did
> 6 saw 7 Have you ever met 8 haven't 9 saw 10 Have you
> ever played 11 have 12 was

b Click on [▭] at the bottom of [2] to play recording 2.10 and students confirm and repeat their answers.

> **TIP:** *After you have opened the audio window it remains open until you close it, so while listening to the audio, just click on* **1** *to look at the start of the exercise and then on* **2** *for the last part.*

Close the flipchart.
Click on ▷ to move to the next double spread.

Double Spread p22/23

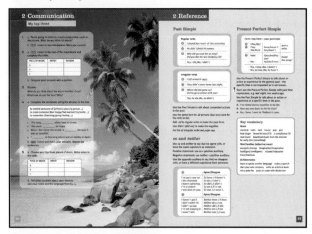

Flipchart: *Special flipchart* **p22**

Before you begin, put students in groups and ask them to think of 5 favourite chocolate bars, 5 favourite films and 5 favourite colours. Ask them to write their suggestions down on a piece of paper and hand it to you. Choose the five most common suggestions.

Open the flipchart by clicking on the circled area and then on the Special Flipchart button ✍☆

On page **1** , write in (using the ✎ tool) the five suggestions under the graph.

Then ask students to conduct a survey in their groups, asking and answering the question 'Which is your favourite _____?' Then, using the ▱ tool, first select the box and then drag the boxes in the graph up, to reflect their findings.

Click on **2** and **3** to find the rest of the exercise

Close the flipchart by clicking X in the toolbar.

Return to the double spread by clicking on the zoomed-up area to make it smaller.

Click on the upwards pointing arrow ▲ to return to Unit 2, and then ▥ to return to the contents page to go to the next module.

Click on **page 25**. It will expand to fill the screen. Remember, you can zoom in to any part of the page by clicking on it, and return by clicking on it again.

Page 25

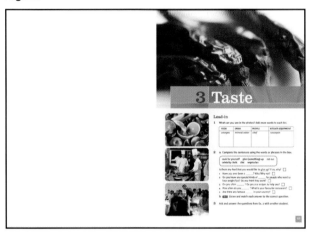

Flipchart: *Lead-in* **p25**

Open the flipchart by clicking on the circled area and then on the flipchart button ⊞.

1 Focus on the photos. Students look at them in pairs and write as many things as they can see in the table in their books. Click on ✎ in the toolbar and ask a student to come to the interactive whiteboard and write their suggestions in the appropriate column.

Click on ▨ to display the answers on a new page.
Click on ◿ to return to ① to compare your answers.

> **ANSWERS**
> FOOD: red chilli peppers (Pic 1), raspberries, lemons, oranges, grapefruits, limes, grapes and apples (Pic 2); DRINK: mineral water (Pic 4); PEOPLE: chef (Pic 3), waiter, customer (Pic 4); KITCHEN EQUIPMENT: cooker, saucepan, frying pan (Pic 3), table, glasses (Pic 4)

Now give the students a few minutes to think in pairs of some more words for each category. Click on a coloured square to change the colour of the pen and have a student come to the interactive whiteboard to add more words to the categories.
Close the flipchart by clicking X in the toolbar.
Return to the double spread by clicking on the zoomed-up area to make it smaller.
Click on ▷ to go to the next double spread.

Double Spread p26/27

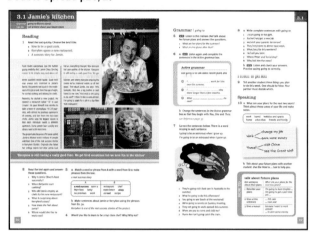

Flipchart: *Reading* **p26**

Open the flipchart.
2 This exercise is on two pages, ① and ② .
Students read the text in their books again slowly and answer the questions in pairs.
Click on ✎ , read out the first question and ask a student to come to the interactive whiteboard to write the answer on the lines for that question. When the student has finished and the class agree, the student can check by clicking on ▨ at the end of the line. Then, that student can read out the next question, nominate another student to come up to continue, and so on. Click on ② to move to the second part of the exercise.

Clicking on ▨ will display the answers below the lines.

> **ANSWERS**
> 1 Because the recipes are simple, easy and tasty. 2 when he was eight 3 unemployed 16–24- year-olds 4 She failed her college exams but then became very successful in Jamie's restaurant. 5 She is very close to Jamie. He's like a big brother or a best friend to her. 6 in a top restaurant in New York

3a Click on ③ . Students work in pairs to match the phrases in their books. Click on ✎ and highlight *recipe* and drill the pronunciation which is often problematic.
Click on ▱ and ask a student to come to the interactive whiteboard to drag the words from the two columns to make phrases from the text in the box below.

> **TIP:** *You can also drag the highlighting itself, but it moves separately.*

Click on ▨ to display the answers on the right.

> **ANSWERS**
> open a restaurant /top-class chef /tasty recipe /no previous experience/ work abroad/

TIP: *For further practice, click on ↺ to go back so the answers are not shown. Click on ✏, drag the slider to increase the width and using green (for example) ask a student to come to the interactive whiteboard and blank out some words of their choice to test the other students. Then students can see if they can remember them. Click on 🧽 and erase the green to reveal the vocabulary again. This can be done slowly to give students spelling clues if they are having difficulty remembering.*

Close the flipchart.

Flipchart: *Grammar* **p27**
Open the flipchart.
7 This exercise is on two pages, [1] and [2].
Focus students' attention on the drawing and read through the example sentence on the interactive whiteboard with the whole group. Tell students to work with a partner to correct the other sentences in their books.
Click on ✏ (maybe use red or green for correction) and ask a student to come to the interactive whiteboard and write their missing word on the line under the sentence, indicating where it should go. After discussion with the whole class, the student can check by clicking on [check] at the end of the line. Then that student can nominate another student to continue, and so on.
Click on [2] to move to the last part of the exercise.

Clicking on [check] will display the answers below the lines.

> **ANSWERS**
> 1 They're going to visit their son in Australia in the summer. 2 What is he going to do this afternoon? 3 Are you going to see Sarah at the weekend? 4 We're going to play tennis on Sunday morning. 5 They're not going to work abroad this summer. 6 When are you going to come and visit me? 7 Marie-Ann isn't going to catch the train.

Close the flipchart.

Flipchart: *Your ideas* **p27**
Open the flipchart by clicking on the circled area and then on the Your Ideas button 📝
Ask students to think about what they are going to do at the weekend. Make notes on their suggestions, using different coloured ✏ tools.
Close the flipchart by clicking X in the toolbar.
Return to the double spread by clicking on the zoomed-up area to make it smaller.
Click on ▶ to go to the next double spread.

Double Spread p28/29

Flipchart: *Pronunciation* **p28**
Open the flipchart.
Focus the students' attention on the extract from the dictionary on the interactive whiteboard, and tell them to pronounce the word with a partner. Ask: Which letter is silent? Click on [check] at the end of the line to display the answer below the line.

> **ANSWER**
> The second 'o'.

Students repeat the word after you.
b In their books, students look at the words in the box with a partner and identify the silent letter. Click on 🧽 and ask a student to come to the interactive whiteboard and highlight the silent letters.
Click on [check] to display the answers.

> **ANSWERS**
> spaghetti, comfortable, Wednesday, vegetable, knife, island, lamb, calm, hour, yoghurt

Close the flipchart.

Flipchart: *Grammar* **p29**
Open the flipchart.
7a Students complete the sentences in their books with a partner. Click on ✏ and ask a student to come to the interactive whiteboard to write *who, which or where* on the lines to complete the sentences. After discussion with the whole class, the student can check by clicking on [check] at the end of the sentence. Then that student can nominate another student to continue, and so on.

Clicking on [check] will display the answers at the end of the lines.

> **ANSWERS**
> 1 where 2 who 3 which 4 where 5 who 6 which 7 who
> 8 where

b In their books, students mark the sentences where *that* is also possible. Click on 🧽 and ask a student to come to the interactive whiteboard and highlight the sentences where *that* could be used. Click on ✏ and write the numbers of those sentences along the line at the bottom.
Click on [check] to display the numbers at the end.

ANSWERS
Sentences 2, 3, 5, 6 and 7.

Close the flipchart.

Flipchart: *Special flipchart* **p29**
Open the flipchart by clicking on the circled area and then on the Special Flipchart button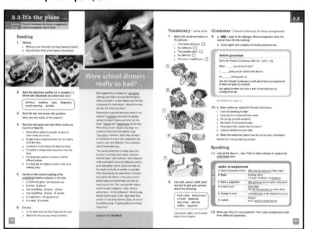
Choose two volunteers to come up to the interactive whiteboard. Ask one student to face away from the board, while the other uses the eraser 🖊 to rub out the black box over one of the pictures. He/She must then describe the picture to his partner, without using the word of the object itself. The second volunteer must guess.
This exercise is over two pages. Click on ② to move on to the second page.
Close the flipchart by clicking X in the toolbar.
Click on ⟫ to go to the next double spread.

Double Spread p30/31

Flipchart: *Your ideas* **p30**
Open the flipchart by clicking on the circled area and then on the Your Ideas button 🖊
Ask students to think about the six headings on the page. Working in groups, ask them to come up with 5-10 food (or drink) items for each heading. Make notes on their suggestions, using different coloured 🖊 tools. Discuss your findings.
Close the flipchart by clicking X in the toolbar.
Return to the double spread by clicking on the zoomed-up area to make it smaller.

Flipchart: *Reading* **p30**
Open the flipchart.
2 Students work in pairs to decide whether the adjectives are negative or positive and if they can use *absolutely* or *very* to modify them. (*absolutely* is used with extreme adjectives, and *very* is used with the moderate adjectives).
Click on 🖊 and ask a student to come to the interactive whiteboard to write in their answers.
Click on ▭ to display the answers on the right.

ANSWERS
+ (absolutely) delicious / – (absolutely) tasteless / + (very) tasty / – (absolutely) disgusting / + (absolutely) mouth-watering / – (absolutely) horrible

TIP: *Click on* 🖊 *to highlight the combinations.*

Close the flipchart.

Flipchart: *Reading* **p30**
Open the flipchart.
4 Read through the sentences on the interactive whiteboard with the whole class, checking that everybody understands. Students then read the text in their books more carefully and work with a partner to say if the statements are true or false. Click on ▱ and ask a student to come to the interactive whiteboard and drag the correct letter, T or F, into the box at the end of each line. Click on ▭ to display the answers after the boxes.

ANSWERS
1 T 2 F 3 T 4 F 5 T 6 F

TIP: *Use* 🖊 *to highlight the correct sentences. Change the thickness of the highlighter with the slider. Click on* 🖊 *and see if students can correct the false sentences.*

Close the flipchart.

Flipchart: *Grammar* **p31**
Open the flipchart.
9a Click on ▦ in the top left corner or at the bottom to play recording 3.7. Students listen to the conversation and check with a partner to decide what arrangement the woman has for that evening.

TIP: *Drag the audio window to a convenient place.*

Click on 🖊 and ask a student to come to the interactive whiteboard to write the arrangement along the line.
Click on ▭ at the end of the line to display the answer below the line.

ANSWER
She's having dinner with Marcin, a friend of her brother's. It's a blind date.

Click on 🖊 to highlight *blind date* on the board and ask they students if they know what it is. Elicit/teach the answer.
b Focus students' attention on the Active grammar box. Play recording 3.7 again and students complete the gaps in their books.
Click on 🖊 and ask a student to come to the interactive whiteboard to write the verbs to complete the sentences.

Click on ▭ to display the verbs at the end of the sentences.

ANSWERS
What are you doing tonight? I'm going out for dinner with Marcin. He's not coming with us.

TIP: *Use* 🖊 *in one colour to highlight be and its examples and another colour to highlight verb+-ing and its examples.*

Point out that the Present Continuous is used to talk about future arrangements. Remind students that in lesson 1.3 they used the Present Continuous to refer to things happening now or around now. Explain that this tense has both functions. Click on the next page button ➡ in the toolbar to move to a blank page. Click on ✏ and write two example sentences on the board: 1 Tonight I'm meeting Sue in the Mexican restaurant. 2 Next year I'm going to learn to drive. Ask students: Which sentence refers to a general plan or intention? (2) What tense do we use? (going to + infinitive) Which sentence tells us where and when the action is going to happen? (1) Which tense do we use? (Present Continuous: be + verb + -ing).

Close the flipchart.
Click on ▷ to go to the next double spread.

Double Spread p32/33

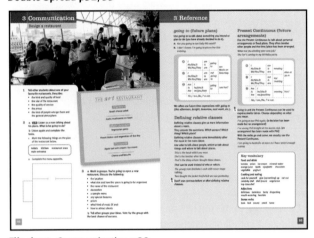

Flipchart: *Communication* **p32**
Open the flipchart.
Click on 🔊 to play recording 3.8 and students listen to answer the question. Students check with a partner.
Click on ✏ and ask a student to come to the interactive whiteboard to write the answer along the line below the picture.
Click on ✓ to display the answer below the line.

> **ANSWER**
> He's going to open a restaurant.

b Click on 2.
Focus students' attention on the floor plan of the restaurant on the interactive whiteboard. Click on 🔊 and play recording 3.8 (first part). Tell the students to listen and, in their books, mark the words from the box on the plan. If necessary, play the recording again.
Click on 🔍 and ask a student to come to the interactive whiteboard to drag the labels from the right onto the correct places on the plan.
Click on ✓ to display the answers on the plan.

> **ANSWERS**
> The kitchen is at the top and the restaurant in the biggest area. The toilets are in the small room (on the left) and the main entrance is opposite.

Click on 3.
Focus students' attention on the menu. Explain the meaning of any of the new words. Click on 🔊 to play recording 3.8 (second part) and students complete the menu in their books. Then students compare answers with a partner.
Click on ✏ and ask a student to come to the interactive whiteboard to write the answer along the lines.

Click on ✓ to display the answers on the right.

> **ANSWERS**
> tomato and orange soup, grilled salmon and new potatoes, chocolate mousse

Close the flipchart.
Click on the upwards pointing arrow ⌃ to return to Unit 3, and then ▥ return to the contents page to go to the next module.

Click on **page 35**. It will expand to fill the screen. Remember, you can zoom in to any part of the page by clicking on it, and return by clicking on it again.

Page 35

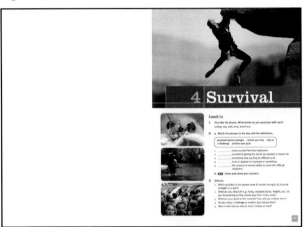

Flipchart: *Lead-in* **p35**

Open the flipchart by clicking on the circled area and then on the flipchart button AV .

2a Check that students understand the words in the box by asking questions: What's the noun of *strong*? What verb goes with *goal* to mean *reach*? Ask other questions as necessary.

Students match the words and phrases in the box to the definitions in their books. Check in pairs.

Click on ⬏ and ask a student to come to the interactive whiteboard to drag the phrases onto the correct line.
You can either check each combination as you work through by clicking on individual ✓ s or check everything together at the end by clicking on the larger ✓ at the bottom.
Clicking on ✓ will display the answers below the boxes.

ANSWERS:
1 control your fear 2 achieve your goal 3 a challenge 4 rely on 5 physical/mental strength

TIP: *For additional practice, click on ↺ to remove the answer boxes, click on ✎, drag the slider in the toolbar to increase the pen width, and blank out all the phrases. Ask students to see if they can remember the new words. Click on 🧽 and slowly erase the pen stroke to reveal the words. (check spelling too).*

Close the flipchart by clicking X in the toolbar.
Return to the double spread by clicking on the zoomed-up area to make it smaller.
Click on ▶ to go to the next double spread.

Double Spread p36/37

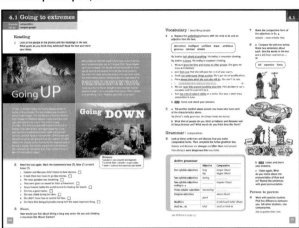

Flipchart: *Reading* **p36**

Open the flipchart.
2 Because of its length, this exercise is on two pages 1 and 2 . Read through the statements with the whole class and check they understand. (Click on 2 to move to the second half of the exercise and then again on 1 to return to the start.) Students read the text in their books again and, in pairs, decide if the sentences are true (T), false (F) or (?) if the answer is not in the text. Students check in pairs.
Click on ✎ and ask a student to come to the interactive whiteboard to write T, F or ? in the boxes.
Depending on your students, you can either check each sentence as you work through by clicking on the individual ✓ s at the end of the lines or check all the sentences together at the end by clicking on ✓ at the bottom. Similarly, you can finish the exercise on 2 before returning to 1 to start checking or check each page as you finish.
Clicking on ✓ will display the answers after the boxes.

ANSWERS:
1 T 2 F 3 T 4 ? 5 ? 6 ? 7 T 8 F 9 T

Ask the students if there are any words or phrases in the text that they don't understand. Encourage students to help each other and answer each other's questions.

TIP: *Click on ✎ to highlight any words in the sentences to clarify for students.*

Close the flipchart.

Flipchart: *Your ideas* **p36**

Open the flipchart by clicking on the circled area and then on the Your Ideas button 🖋
Ask students to talk in groups about any scary/exciting/dangerous activities they may have done. What were they? Make notes or add drawings to the flipchart using the pen tool ✎ . Then discuss, as a class, whether or not students would like to do any of the activities their classmates have mentioned in the future.
Close the flipchart by clicking X in the toolbar.

Return to the double spread by clicking on the zoomed-up area to make it smaller.

Flipchart: *Vocabulary* **p37**

Open the flipchart.

4a This exercise is on 1 and 2. Read the example in the book. with the whole class and tell students to work in pairs to replace the phrases in their books with an adjective from the box and the correct form of the verb to be.

Click on 🖋 and ask a student to come to the interactive whiteboard to erase the phrase in blue. Click on ⤢ and drag the appropriate word from the box into the gap and then click on ✎ and write the correct form of the verb to be. Repeat for each sentence. Click on 2 to do the last part of the exercise and play recording 4.2 so that students can check their answers. Click on ✅ to display the answers in boxes after each sentence.

> **ANSWERS:**
> 1 is generous 2 is confident 3 is intelligent 4 is reliable
> 5 is ambitious 6 is determined 7 is talented

> **TIP:** *Ask various students to read the sentences aloud to check pronunciation and ask them to tell you where the stress is on the new words. Click on ✎ and place a 'blob' above the stressed syllable in the words.*

Close the flipchart

Flipchart: *Special flipchart* **p37**

Open the flipchart by clicking on the circled area and then on the Special Flipchart button ⊞

Use the table as a consolidation exercise. Use the ✎ tool to write in the missing answers into the table.

Close the flipchart by clicking X in the toolbar.

Return to the double spread by clicking on the zoomed-up area to make it smaller.

Click on ⏭ to go to the next double spread.

Double Spread p38/39

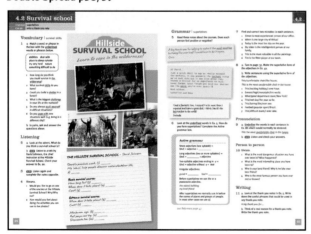

Flipchart: *Listening* **p38**

Open the flipchart.

Focus students' attention on the advert. Elicit ideas on what a survival school is and what you learn there. Click on ✎ and write ideas on the interactive whiteboard but don't confirm or reject anything.

b Ask students to check the ideas on the board as they listen. Click on ⤢ to play recording 4.4. After listening, confirm with students which of the ideas on the board were mentioned. Click on 🖋 and highlight them if appropriate. Click on 2.

3 This exercise is on two pages 2 and 3. Focus on the notes beneath the advert. Establish that students have to complete the notes in their books with information from the listening. Click on ⤢ and play recording 4.4 again. Students check their answers in pairs.

Click on ✎ and ask a student to come to the interactive whiteboard and write on the lines to complete the notes. Ask other students to help if necessary. Click on 3 to finish the exercise before clicking on 2 to return to start checking the answers.

Click on ✅ to display the answers on a new page.

Click on 🔳 to return to 2 to compare your answers. Then click on 3 and check the last part in the same way.

> **ANSWERS:**
> 1 He was in the army. 2 to learn and have fun
> 3 a weekend 4 throughout the year 5 £139 per person
> 6 between November and February 7 £149 per person
> 8 eighteen years old 9 at least four weeks before the
> course begins 10 groups of four or more

Close the flipchart.

Flipchart: *Grammar* **p39**

Open the flipchart.

7 This exercise is on 1 and 2. In their books, students find and correct the mistakes in pairs, then check with a partner. Click on ✎ and ask a student to come to the interactive whiteboard and write the corrections on the lines.

> **TIP:** *Click on 🖋 and highlight the words or areas that need to be corrected. Ask students if they agree.*

You can either check each sentence as you go along, or check at the end of each page or at the end of the exercise. Click on 2 to move to the next page to finish the exercise.

Clicking on ✅ will display the answers below the lines.

> **ANSWERS:**
> 1 Simon is the most experienced person in our office.
> 2 Which is the largest city in Africa. 3 Today is the
> hottest day of the year. 4 My sister is the most intelligent
> person in our family. 5 This is the most valuable of all
> the paintings. 6 Tim is the fittest player in our team.

Close the flipchart.

Flipchart: *Your ideas* **p39**

Open the flipchart by clicking on the circled area and then on the Your Ideas button ⊞

Write a suggested scenario for writing a thank you letter on the flipchart with the ✎ tool (e.g. birthday present, good service, party invitation) Then give students some time to think about what phrases they would use in the letter. Write those on the flipchart with the ✎ and then ask students to write their own letter in their books.

Close the flipchart by clicking X in the toolbar.
Return to the double spread by clicking on the zoomed-up area to make it smaller.
Click on ⏩ to go to the next double spread.

Double Spread p40/41

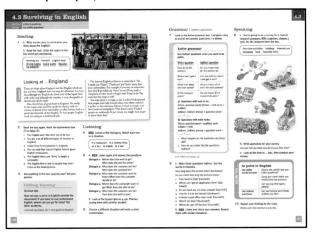

Flipchart: *Listening* **p40**
Open the flipchart.
4 Students look at the names of the places on the interactive whiteboard with a partner and predict sentences they might hear in each place e.g., Can I have the bill? (in a restaurant). Get feedback from different students. Click on ↳ to play recording 4.6. Students listen and match each dialogue to a place in their books and check in pairs.
Click on ✏ and ask a student to come to the interactive whiteboard to write the number of the corresponding dialogue in the boxes. You can either check individually or all together at the end.
Click on ▭ to display the answers next to the boxes.

> **ANSWERS:**
> 1 on a bus 2 in a clothes shop 3 in a bank 4 in a taxi
> 5 in a restaurant

Click on 2 .
5a This exercise is on three pages: dialogue 1 and 2 on 2 , dialogue 3 and 4 on 3 and dialogue 5 on 4 . Read through the questions with the class and then click on ↳ to play recording 4.6 again. Students take notes as they listen and then compare in pairs. If necessary, play the recording again.

> **TIP:** *When you have clicked on ↳ the audio window will open. Click on pause after each dialogue to give students time to write. You can click on 3 or 4 to move to another page while the audio is playing and the audio will continue.*

Click on ✏ and ask a student to come to the interactive whiteboard to write the answers along the lines. You can either check individually, page by page or at the end. Click on 3 to move to page 3 and 4 to move to page 4.
Click on ▭ to display the answers below the lines.

> **ANSWERS:**
> 1 Carson Street. How much is it?/Can you tell me how long it takes? 2 a size 12, the assistant has a look 3 how much they charge to change euros into pounds, to change 200 euros 4 Queens Road, near Victoria station. She offers to tell the taxi driver where to go when they get nearer. 5 the bill, by credit card (Mastercard)

b Students work in pairs to practise the conversations, using the tapescript as a guide. After they have read through it once, students can be given freer practice by repeating the conversations but with only one of them looking at the tapescript and the other student improvising.

> **TIP:** *It's convenient to drill some of the language from the conversations. Drag the slider in the audio window back a little to repeat the last few words. Hold the slider to pause while students repeat, and then drag it forward to locate the next part you would like to drill.*

Close the flipchart.

Flipchart: *Grammar* **p41**
Open the flipchart.
8a This exercise is on 1 and 2 .
Students work in pairs to make the questions indirect like the example in their books.
Click on ✏ and ask a student to come to the interactive whiteboard to write the indirect questions along the corresponding lines. Click on 2 to finish the exercise before clicking on ↳ on 2 to play recording 4.7 so that students can check their answers.
Clicking on ▭ will display the answers below the lines.

> **ANSWERS:**
> 1 Can you tell me how much that is? 2 Do you know where I can get an application form? 3 Can you tell me if you have any 1st class stamps? 4 Do you know how far it is to the library? 5 Can you tell me if there's a post office near here? 6 Do you know what the time is? 7 Can you tell me where I get off the bus?

Click on ↳ to play recording 4.7 again, pausing after each question to allow students to repeat with the correct intonation. Then ask them to practise with a partner.

> **TIP:** *Click on the slider in the audio window and hold it to pause the recording while students repeat. Then release to continue. Alternatively, you can click on pause and then play.*

Close the flipchart.
Click on the upwards pointing arrow ▣ to return to Unit 4, and then ▣ to return to the contents page to go to the next module.

Click **page 45**. It will expand to fill the screen. Remember, you can zoom in to any part of the page by clicking on it, and return by clicking on it again.

Page 45

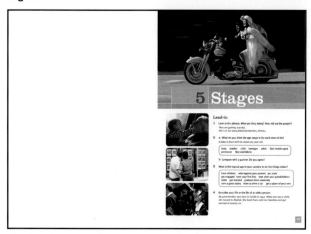

Flipchart: *Lead-in* **p45**
Open the flipchart by clicking on the circled area and then on the flipchart button AV.
2a Check that students understand the words in the column.
Q: When you are six months old, what are you? (a baby) Q: When you are two years old, what are you? (a toddler) and so on. Tell the students to write an age range for each word individually.
b Have students compare with a partner to see if they agree or disagree with each other.
Click on ✏ and ask a student to come to the interactive whiteboard and write the age ranges in the column on the right and then discuss each concept with the whole class.
Click on [✓ CHECK] to display the answers on the right.

> **ANSWERS:**
> baby: 0 to 1; toddler: 1 to 4; child: 2 to 16; teenager: 13 to 19; adult: 18+; (be) middle-aged: 40 to 60; pensioner: 60-65+; (be) old/elderly: 70+

> **TIP:** *Click on* 🔲 *and drag the cover to the left to cover the words. See if students can remember. Click on* 🔲 *again to remove the cover and reveal the words.*

Close the flipchart by clicking X in the toolbar.
Return to the double spread by clicking on the zoomed-up area to make it smaller.

Flipchart: *Your ideas* **p45**
Open the flipchart by clicking on the circled area and then on the Your Ideas button AV.
Ask students to look at the ideas on the flipchart. Put them into groups and ask them to think about the ages at which those things can be done.
Make notes on the board, using the ✏ tool.
Close the flipchart by clicking X in the toolbar.

Return to the double spread by clicking on the zoomed-up area to make it smaller.
Click on ⟩⟩ to go to the next double spread.

Double Spread p46/47

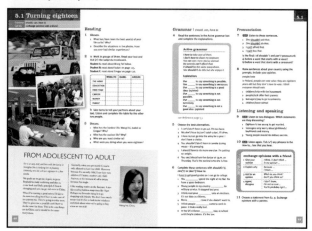

Flipchart: *Grammar* **p47**
Open the flipchart.
Students work in pairs to choose the best alternative in their books.
Click on 🖊 and ask a student to come to the interactive whiteboard and erase the incorrect choice to leave the best alternative. You can either check each sentence as you work through by clicking on the [✓ CHECK]s at the end of each line or check all the sentences together at the end by clicking on [✓ CHECK] at the bottom.
Clicking on [✓ CHECK] will highlight the answers.

> **ANSWERS:**
> 1 can't 2 don't have to 3 have to 4 shouldn't 5 should 6 can

Click on ②.
6 Read the example sentence in their books with the whole class and then students work in pairs to complete the rest of the sentences. Click on ✏ and ask a student to come to the interactive whiteboard to write the correct choice along the lines provided.
Click on [✓ CHECK] to display the answers at the ends of the sentences.

> **ANSWERS:**
> 1 can 2 don't have to 3 should 4 doesn't have to
> 5 shouldn't 6 have to

Close the flipchart.

Flipchart: *Special flipchart* **p47**
Open the flipchart by clicking on the circled area and then on the Special Flipchart button AV
Using the How To box on the left of the flipchart, ask students to choose a topic to talk about. Put the students in pairs and ask them to take opposing sides of the argument (and then swap).

Make notes on what phrases and points of argument they use.
Close the flipchart by clicking X in the toolbar.
Return to the double spread by clicking on the zoomed-up area to make it smaller.
Click on ▷ to go to the next double spread.

Double Spread p48/49

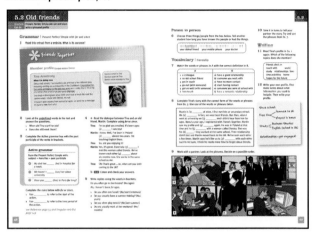

Flipchart: *Grammar* **p48**
Open the flipchart.
4a Students work in pairs to complete the dialogue in their books.
b Click on ⏵ to play recording 5.3 and students check their answers.

> **TIP:** *Drag the audio window to a convenient place so that it is not covering any of the text.*

Click on ⬏ and ask a student to come to the interactive whiteboard to drag the correct choice of *for* or *since* from the top into the gaps.
Click on ▭ to display the answers below the lines.

> **ANSWERS:**
> 1 since 2 for 3 since 4 for

Click on ⬛ .
5 Read through the example question in their books, prompt and answer with the whole class, and then students work in pairs to write the replies. Click on ✎ and ask a student to come to the interactive whiteboard to write the answers along the lines.
Click on ▭ to display the answers below the lines.

> **ANSWERS:**
> 1 No, I haven't seen her since last Christmas. 2 No, I haven't had a summer holiday for years. 3 No, I haven't played since last summer. 4 No, I haven't worked at the weekend for months.

> **TIP:** *Click on ✎ to highlight expressions with for and since.*

Close the flipchart.

Flipchart: *Vocabulary* **p49**
Open the flipchart.
7 Students work with a partner to match items from each column with the definitions in their books. Click on ⬏ and ask a student to come to the interactive whiteboard and drag the definitions on

the right up and down in their column so that they match the words on the left.
Click on ▭ to display the answers on a new page.
Click on ⬛ to return to ⬛ to compare your answers.

> **ANSWERS:**
> 1 b) 2 e) 3 d) 4 f) 5 a) 6 c)

> **TIP:** *On the answer page, click on ✎ , drag the slider on the toolbar to a thick width and blank out the words on the left. See if students can remember them. Click on ✎ and ask a student to come to the interactive whiteboard and check the blanked out words. Ask them to erase slowly if necessary, to give clues to help with spelling.*

Close the flipchart.

Flipchart: *Vocabulary* **p49**
Open the flipchart.
9 Focus students' attention on the pictures on the interactive whiteboard and explain the task. Tell students to work in pairs and put the pictures in order in their books.
Click on ⬏ and ask a student to come to the interactive whiteboard to drag the pictures into the correct order. Get feedback from various students to see if everybody agrees. It's fine if some students have a different order as long as they can justify its logic.
Click on ▭ to display the suggested order in a box at the bottom.

> **SUGGESTED ANSWER:**
> D, C, A, E, B

> **TIP:** *After the students have practised in exercise 10, ask for a volunteer come out to use the pictures on the interactive whiteboard to retell the story. Click on ✎ and annotate the pictures with the appropriate vocabulary from exercise 7.*

Close the flipchart.
Click on ▷ to go to the next double spread.

Double Spread p50/51

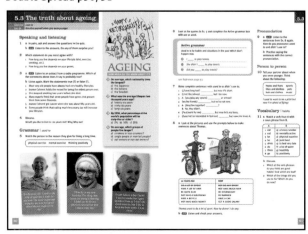

Flipchart: *Speaking and Listening* **p50**
Open the flipchart.

1a This exercise is on two pages ⬛1 and ⬛2 . Focus students on the Ageing quiz and tell them to answer the questions in their books in pairs. Get feedback and discuss points that students do not agree on, but don't give them the correct answers yet. Click on ⬛2 .
b Click on 🔘 to play recording 5.4 and students check their answers. Click on ⬛1 , click on ✏ and ask a student to come to the interactive whiteboard to highlight the correct answers on both pages.
Click on ⬛✓✓ to highlight the answers.

ANSWERS:
1 The Japanese 2 twenty-six years 3 20%
4a) non-smokers b) married people c) pet owners

Ask the students if anything has surprised them and discuss why. Close the flipchart.

Flipchart: *Grammar* **p50**
Open the flipchart.
5 Focus the students on the three phrases in the box. Ask them how much each factor contributes to reaching an old age. Q: Do you think physical exercise is very important if you want to live a long time? Q: Is mental exercise as important as physical exercise? Q: How important is thinking positively?
Now students read the quotes under the pictures in pairs and match a phrase to each one in their books. Click on ⬅ and ask a student to come to the interactive whiteboard to drag the reasons from the box onto the line below the appropriate picture.
Click on ⬛✓✓ to display the answers below the lines.

ANSWERS:
Text 1: thinking positively Text 2: physical exercise Text 3: mental exercise

TIP: *Click on ✏ and using a thick width, blank out the three reasons. Change the pen width back to normal and ask a student to come to the interactive whiteboard and write in the missing words. Click on ⬅ , click on the 'blanks' and drag them to reveal the words.*

OPTIONAL GRAMMAR LEAD-IN: Tell the students look at the quotes on the interactive whiteboard for one minute and try to remember what the people say. Tell them to close their books and ask the following questions: The first man believes in thinking positively, but what did he use to do? Elicit: *sport.* The woman dances now, but did she use to do physical exercise? Elicit: No, she didn't. What did the second man use to do when he was younger? Elicit: *smoke.* Click on ✏ and highlight these words.
Close the flipchart.

Flipchart: *Vocabulary* **p51**
Open the flipchart.
11a Students work in pairs to match the verb and noun phrases in their books. Click on ⬅ and ask a student to come to the interactive whiteboard to drag the noun phrases on the right up and down until they correspond to the correct verb.
Click on ⬛✓✓ to display the answers on a new page.
Click on ⬛ to return to ⬛1 to compare your answers.

ANSWERS:
eat junk food/ eat healthily; be mentally active/ be a heavy smoker; drink a lot of water; do physical exercise; think positively; go to bed very late

Click on ⬛2 .
b Students discuss the first question in small groups. Click on ✏ and ask a student to come to the interactive whiteboard to write their group's suggestions along the lines provided.
Click on ⬛✓✓ to display the answers to 1 below the last line.

ANSWERS:
Good habits: eat healthily, be mentally active, drink a lot of water, do physical exercise, think positively
Bad habits: eat junk food, be a heavy smoker, go to bed very late.

Ask students to discuss the second question in small groups and then ask for volunteers to come to the interactive whiteboard and write some example sentences on the lines provided. You could return to the Answers page from ⬛1 and do a class survey comparing the past and now. (Blank out one of the alternatives for *be* and *eat.*)
Close the flipchart.

Double Spread p56/57

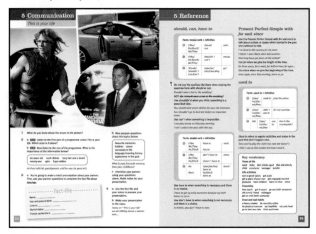

Flipchart: *Your ideas* **p52**
Students look at p62 in their books and see if they recognise the film stars pictured there.
Then, open the flipchart by clicking on the circled area and then on the Your Ideas button 🔳 . Here you will see the names of the celebrities at the top of the page and space underneath for note-making. Ask your students what they know about the actors and make notes with the ✏ tool. If the students don't know very much, then ask them to suggest some questions one could ask the actors instead.
Close the flipchart by clicking X in the toolbar.
Return to the double spread by clicking on the zoomed-up area to make it smaller.
Click on the upwards pointing arrow 🔼 to return to Unit 5, and then 🔳 to return to the contents page to go to the next module.

Click **page 55**. It will expand to fill the screen. Remember, you can zoom in to any part of the page by clicking on it, and return by clicking on it again.

Page 55

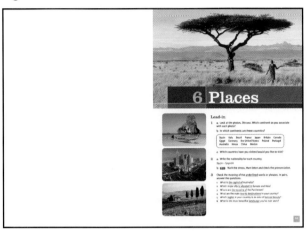

Flipchart: *Lead-in* **p55**

Open the flipchart by clicking on the circled area and then on the flipchart button.

1a Focus students' attention on the photos on the interactive whiteboard and tell them to work in pairs to guess which continent each photo was taken in.

Click on and ask a student to come to the interactive whiteboard to write the names of the continents on the lines below the pictures. Discuss and see if all the class agree.

Click on to display the answers below the lines.

> **ANSWERS:**
> Pic 1: Africa Pic 2: Asia
> Pic 3: North America. Pic 4: Europe

Elicit the continents that are not shown in the photos (South America, Antarctica, the Arctic and Australasia). Click on and write them at the side.

> **TIP:** *Click on , check pronunciation and elicit the number of syllables. Place a 'blob' above the stressed syllable.*

Click on 2 .

b Tell students to work in pairs to say which continent each country in the box at the bottom belongs to. Check pronunciation of the countries before students begin. (But don't highlight stress before the words are dragged or you will have to go back and drag the 'blobs' too.)

Click on and ask a student to come to the interactive whiteboard to drag the names of the countries into the correct column. Ask them to say the name as they drag it. Click on to display the answers on a new page.

Click on to return to 1 to compare your answers.

> **ANSWERS:**
> Africa: Egypt, Kenya. Asia: Japan, China. Australasia: Australia. Europe: Spain, Italy, France, Germany, Poland, Portugal, Britain. North America: Canada, Mexico, the United States.

Click on to mark stress on the Answers page.
Close the flipchart by clicking X in the toolbar.
Return to the double spread by clicking on the zoomed-up area to make it smaller.

Flipchart: *Your ideas* **p55**

Open the flipchart by clicking on the circled area and then on the Your Ideas button

Ask students to think about which countries they have visited, and which countries they would like to visit. Ask them for their reasons and make notes, using the tool.

Close the flipchart by clicking X in the toolbar.
Return to the double spread by clicking on the zoomed-up area to make it smaller.

Click on to go to the next double spread.

Double Spread p56/57

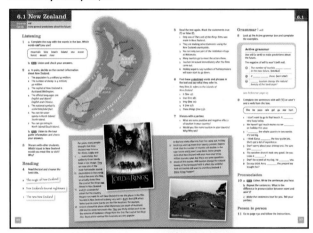

Flipchart: *Listening* **p56**

Open the flipchart.

1a Students work with a partner to label the map in their books. Clarify the pronunciation of *island*.

b Click on to play recording 6.2 and students listen and check their answers.

Click on and ask a student to come to the interactive whiteboard to label the map by dragging the place names next to the numbers on the map.

Click on to display the answers on the right at the bottom.

> **ANSWERS:**
> 1 beach 2 mountain 3 sea 4 ocean 5 river 6 lake 7 island. All the words are used except forest and desert.

Click on 2 .

2a Students discuss the sentences in pairs and guess what information is correct.

b Click on to play recording 6.3 and students check their answers.

Click on and ask a student to come to the interactive whiteboard to erase the incorrect information in the sentences.

> **TIP:** *If students make a mistake, click on the Undo button in the toolbar to delete the last stroke. Change the width of the eraser by dragging the slider in the toolbar.*

Click on ⬚ to highlight the answers.

ANSWERS:
1 4 million 2 40 million 3 Wellington 4 English and Maori
5 kiwi bird 6 North Island 7 South Island

Ask a number of students to read the correct sentences aloud.
Close the flipchart.

Flipchart: *Grammar* **p57**
Open the flipchart.
9 This exercise is on two pages ⬚ and ⬚ . Check the students
understand all the verbs in the box at the top and then ask them
to work in pairs to complete the sentences in their books. Click on
⬚ and ask a student to come to the interactive whiteboard to
drag the correct verb onto each line. Click on ⬚ and write *will* or
won't to complete the sentence. You can either check each
sentence as you finish it by clicking on ⬚ at the end of the
line or all together for that page by clicking on ⬚ at the
bottom. Similarly, you can check each page as you finish or click
on ⬚ , finish the exercise and then click on ⬚ to return and
check all together at the end.
Clicking on ⬚ will display the answers below the lines.

ANSWERS:
1 will be 2 won't go 3 won't see 4 will get 5 will pass
6 will rain 7 won't hurt 8 will like

Close the flipchart.
Click on ⬚ to go to the next double spread.

Double Spread p58/59

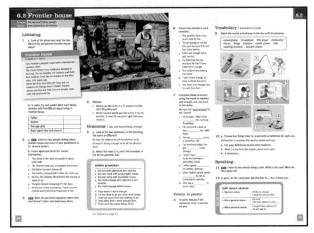

Flipchart: *Grammar* **p58**
Open the flipchart.
5a Students discuss the question with a partner. Click on ⬚ and
ask a student to come to the interactive whiteboard to drag the
correct word onto the line.
Click on ⬚ to display the answer below the line.

ANSWER:
same

Click on ⬚ .
b Students match the examples and the rules in their books. Click
on ⬚ and ask a student to come to the interactive whiteboard to
drag the example sentences on the right up and down until they
match the rules on the left.

Click on ⬚ to display the answers on the right.

ANSWERS:
1 B – I'm too tired to do any more work today. 2 C – I had
too much time and nothing to do. 3 E – There were too
many things to do. 4 A – They weren't warm enough.
5 D – They often didn't have enough food.

TIP: *Click on* ⬚ *and highlight the key language in the*
examples.

Tell the students to look at Reference page 63. Give them a
moment to read through the notes and then ask: What's the
difference between *too* and *very*? (*Too* is used with a problem and
very when something is difficult but not impossible.) Click on ⬚ ,
click on ⬚ and write the following sentences on the board and
ask the students to discuss the difference in pairs. Elicit/teach the
difference. This coffee is very sweet. (No opinion is expressed)
This coffee is too sweet. (A negative opinion is expressed)
Close the flipchart.

Flipchart: *Grammar* **p59**
Open the flipchart.
7 This exercise is on ⬚ and ⬚ . Read the example together in
the book and tell students to complete the sentences in pairs.
Click on ⬚ and ask a student to come to the interactive
whiteboard and write on the lines to complete the sentences.
Click on ⬚ to display the answers below the lines.

ANSWERS:
1 I'm hungry. I didn't have <u>enough breakfast</u> this morning.
2 I'm very tired. I went to bed <u>too late</u> last night. 3 I'm not
<u>fit enough</u> to run a marathon. 4 I'm very busy today. I've
got <u>too many things</u> to do. 5 I didn't have <u>enough time</u> to
do my homework yesterday. 6 I often spend <u>too much</u>
<u>money</u> on clothes. 7 Most English people speak <u>too quickly</u>
for me to understand. 8 This tea is <u>too hot</u> to drink.

TIP: *Click on* ⬚ *, click on* ⬚ *and highlight a keyword in each*
sentence and tell students they should try to memorize the four
sentences they see. Then click on ⬚ *to cover the sentences,*
give the keywords as prompts and see if students can
remember the complete sentence. Click on ⬚ *again to reveal*
the sentences and repeat for ⬚ *.*

Close the flipchart.

Flipchart: *Vocabulary* **p59**
Open the flipchart.
9 This exercise is on ⬚ and ⬚ . Check pronunciation of the
words in the box. Students work in pairs to match the words and
the pictures in their books. Click on ⬚ and ask a student to come
to the interactive whiteboard to label the pictures by dragging the
words from the box onto the pictures.
Click on ⬚ to display the answers above, below and next to
the pictures.

ANSWERS:
A mobile phone B answerphone C vacuum cleaner
D hairdryer E dishwasher F washing machine G fridge
H freezer I DVD player J radio K CD-walkman

TIP: *Repeat this exercise later, but cover the vocabulary. On* 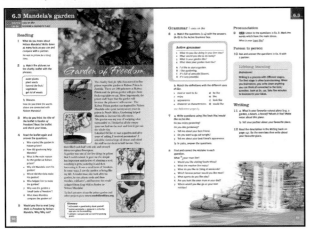... no

TIP: *Repeat this exercise later, but cover the vocabulary. On* 1*, click on* ▬ *and drag the cover up to reveal the pictures but keep the vocabulary hidden. Click on* ✏ *, and ask a student to come to the interactive whiteboard to write the words on the pictures. Click on* 2 *and repeat, and then click on* ▭ *to check.*

Close the flipchart.

Flipchart: *Special flipchart* **p59**

Open the flipchart by clicking on the circled area and then on the Special Flipchart button 📄

This exercise asks students to be creative! Working in pairs, ask students to discuss the five things they would take to a desert island, and why. They can use the How To box for help. When they have finished this task, ask a volunteer to come up to the interactive whiteboard and give a demonstration of their choices, using the ✏ tool to make notes.

Close the flipchart by clicking X in the toolbar.

Return to the double spread by clicking on the zoomed-up area to make it smaller.

Click on ▶ to go to the next double spread.

Double Spread p60/61

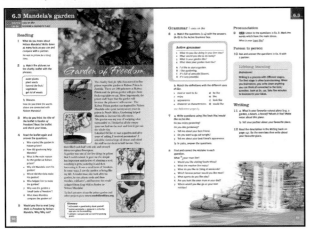

Flipchart: *Your ideas* **p60**

Open the flipchart by clicking on the circled area and then on the Your Ideas button 📄

Ask students to get into small groups and discuss what they know about Nelson Mandela. Move around and give them some clues if they seem to be struggling.

Make notes on the flipchart with the pen tool ✏.

Close the flipchart by clicking X in the toolbar.

Return to the double spread by clicking on the zoomed-up area to make it smaller.

Flipchart: *Grammar* **p61**

Open the flipchart.

8 This exercise is on 1 and 2. Read the example in their books and tell students to work in pairs to find and correct the mistakes.

Click on ✏ and ask a student to come to the interactive whiteboard, choose a colour for the pen and write the corrected question on the lines. You can either check each sentence as you finish it by clicking on ▭ at the end of the line or all together for that page by clicking on ▭ at the bottom. Similarly, you can check each page as you finish or click on 2, finish the

exercise and then click on 1 to return and check all together at the end

Clicking on ▭ will display the answers below the lines.

ANSWERS:

1 Would you like to visit South Africa? 2 What is the weather like today? 3 What do you like doing at weekends? 4 Which famous person would you like to meet? 5 What sports do you like playing? 6 Do you look like your mum or your dad? 7 Where would you like to go on your next holiday?

TIP: *Click on* ✏ *, select red as the colour and mark X on the incorrect part of the sentence.*

Close the flipchart.

Flipchart: *Pronunciation* **p61**

Open the flipchart.

9a Explain to the students that when we ask a question we usually only stress the most important words. Focus them on the example in their books and then ask them to look back at Ex. 8 and tell them to listen to the sentences and underline the words which are stressed the most. Click on 🔊 to play recording 6.8.

TIP: *Drag the audio window to a convenient place.*

Pause and repeat as necessary for your students. Students check in pairs.

Click on ✏ and ask a student to come to the interactive whiteboard to highlight the words that are stressed. You can either check each sentence as you work through by clicking on ▭ at the end of each line or check all the sentences together at the end.

Click on ▭ to highlight the answers.

ANSWERS:

1 Would you like to visit South Africa? 2 What is the weather like today? 3 What do you like doing at weekends? 4 Which famous person would you like to meet? 5 What sports do you like playing? 6 Do you look like your mum or your dad? 7 Where would you like to go on your next holiday?

Close the flipchart. Click on the upwards pointing arrow 🔼 to return to Unit 6, and then 🔲 to return to the contents page to go to the next module.

Click **page 65**. It will expand to fill the screen. Remember, you can zoom in to any part of the page by clicking on it, and return by clicking on it again.

Page 65

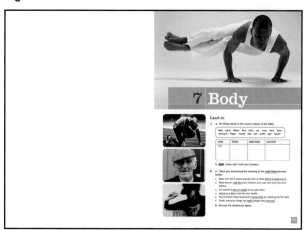

Flipchart: *Lead-in* **p65**

Open the flipchart by clicking on the circled area and then on the flipchart button `AV`.

1a Students work in pairs to categorise the words for parts of the body in their books. Tell them to practise saying the words as they do this and go around the class checking pronunciation.

b Click on 🔘 to play recording 7.1 so that the students can check their answers. Now check that students know the exact meaning of any new words by telling them to point to these body parts or have different students give these instructions.

Click on ⬉ and ask a student to come to the interactive whiteboard to drag the words from the box at the top into the correct column.

Click on ⬜ to display the answers at the bottom of each column.

> **ANSWERS:**
> HEAD: hair, face, ear, nose, lips, eye, mouth TORSO: waist, back, stomach ARM/HAND: elbow, wrist, finger, thumb LEG/FOOT: knee, toe, ankle

Close the flipchart by clicking X in the toolbar.
Return to the double spread by clicking on the zoomed-up area to make it smaller.
Click on ⬛ to go to the next double spread.

Double Spread p66/67

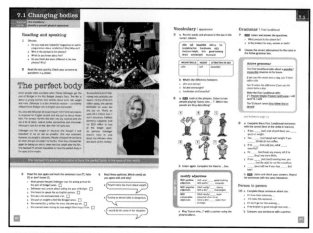

Flipchart: *Reading and speaking* **p66**
Open the flipchart.

3 Read the statements on the interactive whiteboard with the whole class and then tell students to read the text again in their books and to mark each statement true (T), false (F) or (?) if the answer is not given in the text. Ask students to compare answers with a partner.
Click on ✏ and ask a student to come to the interactive whiteboard to put T, F or ? in the boxes. You can either click on ⬜ at the ends of each line to check answers consecutively, or click on ⬜ at the bottom to check all the answers together. Clicking on ⬜ will display the answers next to the boxes.

> **ANSWERS:**
> 1 T 2 ? 3 T 4 F 5 ? 6 F 7 T

Ask students if they have any vocabulary problems with the text and encourage other students to explain any words before doing so yourself.
Close the flipchart.

Flipchart: *Grammar* **p67**
Open the flipchart.

7 Tell the students they are going to listen to a radio advert. Read the questions on the interactive whiteboard with the class. Click on 🔘 to play recording 7.3. Students write in their books and compare in pairs. Click on ✏ and ask a student to come to the interactive whiteboard to write the answers on the lines.
Click on ⬜ to display the answers below the lines.

> **ANSWERS:**
> 1 'Face Saver' face cream
> 2 men

Click on `2`.
Tell students to read through the Active grammar box in their books and choose the correct alternatives. Students compare in pairs. Click on 🖊 and ask a student to come to the interactive whiteboard to erase the incorrect alternatives for the rules.
Click on ⬜ to highlight the answers.

> **ANSWERS:**
> The First Conditional talks about a possible situation in the future. The if clause comes either first or second.

Refer students to Reference page 73 and give them time to read through the notes. To check comprehension, ask: Can we use will in the if clause? (No) When do we need to use a comma? (if the if clause comes first). What other types of verbs can we use instead of will? (modals such as *could*, *may* and *might*). Click on ✎ and highlight these points.

Close the flipchart.

Click on ⏩ to go to the next double spread.

Double Spread p68/69

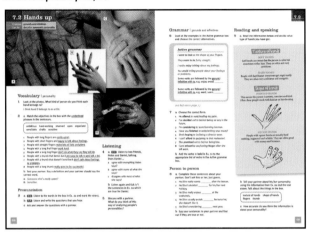

Flipchart: *Vocabulary* p68

Open the flipchart.

1 This exercise is on [1] and [2]. Focus students' attention on the photos on the interactive whiteboard and tell them to discuss the question in pairs. Click on ✎ and ask a student to come to the interactive whiteboard to write suggestions next to the pictures. Get feedback from the whole class.

Click on [2] for pictures C and D and repeat.

Close the flipchart.

Flipchart: *Listening* p68

Open the flipchart.

4a Tell students they are going to listen to two people talking about how you can predict personality by looking at somebody's hands. Focus them on the question about Daniel, click on 🔊 and play recording 7.7. Students check in pairs. Click on ✎ and ask a student to come to the interactive whiteboard to highlight the correct alternative.

Click on ▭ to highlight the answer.

> **ANSWER:**
> a

Click on [2].

b This exercise is on [2] and [3]. Click on 🔊 to play recording 7.7 again and, in their books, students tick the sentences in Ex. 2a which are true for Daniel. Students check in pairs. Click on ✎ and ask a student to come to the interactive whiteboard and tick the boxes after the true sentences for Daniel. Click on [3] to finish the exercise. You can either check each page as you finish or click on [3], finish the exercise and then click on [2] to return and check from the beginning.

Click on ▭ to display the answers after the boxes.

> **ANSWERS:**
> The true sentences are 2, 3, 6 and 8.

> **TIP:** *You may want to revise the vocabulary from Exercise 2a by clicking on* ✎*, asking students if they can remember the adjectives, and writing them in. Ask students to give the spelling too.*

Close the flipchart.

Flipchart: *Person to person* p69

Open the flipchart.

8a Divide the class into pairs and students complete the sentences in their books about their partner. They cannot speak at this stage. Go around the room monitoring their work.

b Students speak to their partner to find out if they were right. If students were wrong they have to change the sentence. Give an example yourself with one student e.g., 'I think you want to move to England next year.' 'No, I don't.' 'What do you want to do?' 'I want to finish university.' Click on ✎ and ask a student to come to the interactive whiteboard and write an example sentence about their partner. Ask them to write the name of their partner instead of He/She at the beginning.

Close the flipchart.

Click on ⏩ to go to the next double spread.

Double Spread p70/71

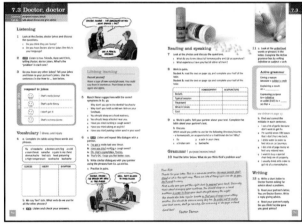

Flipchart: *Vocabulary* p70

Open the flipchart.

4a Focus the students on the chart on the interactive whiteboard and read the headings with the whole class.

> **TIP:** *Click on* ✎ *and mark the stressed syllable. Try and elicit the number of syllables and the stress from the students first.*

In pairs, students put the vocabulary items into the correct category in their books. Check pronunciation, paying particular attention to the pronunciation of *ache*. Tell students that some items could go into more than one category. Students check in pairs.

Click on ⬐ and ask a student to come to the interactive whiteboard to drag the words from the box at the top into the correct column.

b Students answer the question in pairs. Click on ✎ and ask a student to come to the interactive whiteboard and write the verb on the line. (The answer is *have*, although we could also use *get* with all the others except for a broken arm/leg).

c Click on 🔊 to play recording 7.9. Students listen to check their answers. Click on ▭ to display the answers on a new page. Click on ▭ to return to [1] to compare your answers.

> **ANSWERS:**
> ILLNESS: flu, a cold, food poisoning INJURY: a broken
> arm/leg SYMPTOM: a headache, a sore throat, earache,
> a pain in my chest, stomachache, feel sick, a high
> temperature, toothache, backache

Click on 2 .

5 Read the example sentence in their books with the whole class
and then ask students to work in pairs to match the symptoms
and suggestions. Go around the class helping with any difficult
vocabulary.
Click on 🔺 and ask a student to come to the interactive
whiteboard to drag the symptom from the box onto the line next
to the appropriate suggestion.
Click on [CHECK] to display the answers below the lines.

> **ANSWERS:**
> 1 a high temperature 2 backache 3 feel sick 4 a sore
> throat 5 a headache 6 earache

> **TIP:** *For further practice, on 2 , click on ✏ and highlight the*
> *symptoms for which there were suggestions. Click on ▦ and*
> *drag the cover down to show the symptoms. Ask one student*
> *to describe his problem, using the correct verb and see if*
> *another student can remember the suggestion. Then drag the*
> *cover down to reveal the suggestions.*

Close the flipchart.

Flipchart: *Special flipchart* **p70**
Open the flipchart by clicking on the circled area and then on the
Special Flipchart button 🔲
Put the class into pairs of similar ability. Student A needs to
imagine that they have a medical problem, and describe their
symptoms to B. Model this on the flipchart with the pen tool ✏ .
Student B then looks at the medicine cabinet on the interactive
whiteboard and chooses the appropriate medicine. A and B then
swap positions.
Close the flipchart by clicking X in the toolbar.
Return to the double spread by clicking on the zoomed-up area to
make it smaller.

Flipchart: *Your ideas* **p71**
Open the flipchart by clicking on the circled area and then on the
Your Ideas button 🔲
Ask students to think about 'alternative medicine'. Allow them to
look up the phrase in the dictionary if necessary. First, they should
suggest some different types of alternative medicine and then
make lists of the good and bad points of each one if they can.
Collate ideas on the interactive whiteboard, using the pen tool ✏ .
Close the flipchart by clicking X in the toolbar.
Return to the double spread by clicking on the zoomed-up area to
make it smaller.

Flipchart: *Grammar* **p71**
Open the flipchart.
11a Focus the students' attention on the Active grammar box on
the interactive whiteboard. In pairs, they read the examples and
complete the rules in their books. Click on ✏ and ask a student
to come to the interactive whiteboard to write on the lines to
complete the patterns.

Click on [CHECK] to display the answers on the right.

> **ANSWERS:**
> so + <u>subject</u> + <u>verb</u>
> in order (not) to + <u>infinitive</u>
> so that + <u>subject</u> + <u>verb</u>

Tell the students to look at Reference page 73. Give them a
moment to read through the notes and ask: How do we express
purpose in formal situations? (in order to)
Click on 2 .
b This exercise is on 2 and 3 . Students work in pairs to correct
the sentences in their books. Click on ✏ and ask a student to
come to the interactive whiteboard and write the correction above
the sentences.
You can either click on [CHECK] at the ends of each line to check
answers consecutively, or click on [CHECK] at the bottom to check
all the answers together.
Alternatively, you can click on 3 and finish the exercise and then
return to 2 to check each page.
Clicking on [CHECK] will display the answers below the sentences.

> **ANSWERS:**
> 1 I eat a lot of garlic because <u>I</u> don't want to get flu. 2 I'm
> careful when I lift boxes <u>so</u> that I don't hurt my back. 3 I
> drink water in order <u>not</u> to feel sick on car journeys. 4 I
> did a lot of yoga today so <u>I</u> feel very relaxed now. 5 I want
> to buy a special chair <u>to</u> help me sit properly. 6 I usually
> drink milk <u>in</u> order to get rid of a stomachache.

> **TIP:** *Click on ✏ , select red as the colour and mark X on the*
> *incorrect part of the sentence.*

Close the flipchart.

Double Spread p68/69

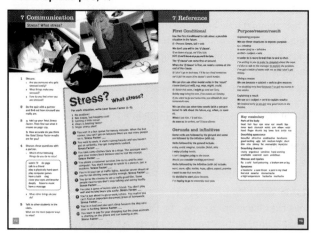

Flipchart: *Your ideas* **p72**
Open the flipchart by clicking on the circled area and then on the
Your Ideas button 🔲
Write the word STRESS on the board using ✏ . Explain the idea if
students are not already aware of stress. Collate ideas about what
causes stress and how it shows itself. Encourage the class to talk
in groups and compare their experiences.
Close the flipchart by clicking X in the toolbar.
Return to the double spread by clicking on the zoomed-up area to
make it smaller.
Click on the upwards pointing arrow 🔼 to return to Unit 7, then
🔲 to return to the contents page to go to the next module.

Unit 8

Click on the **double spread p76/77**. It will expand to fill the screen. Remember, you can zoom in to any part of the page by clicking on it, and return by clicking on it again.

Double Spread p76/77

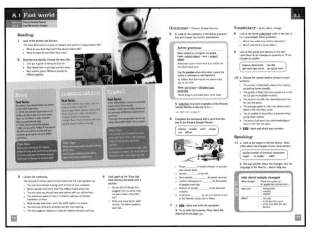

Flipchart: *Reading* **p76**
Open the flipchart by clicking on the circled area and then on the flipchart button AV.
1 Focus students on the photos and explanation on the interactive whiteboard and explain what the Slow Movement is. Tell students to discuss and answer the two questions in pairs. Click on 🖊 and ask a student to come to the interactive whiteboard to write their answers on the lines provided.
Click on 2 .
2 Students read through the text in their books quickly and choose the best title. Tell them not to worry about any vocabulary they don't understand at this stage. Students check in pairs. Click on 🖊 and ask a student to come to the interactive whiteboard to highlight the best title.
Click on ☐ to highlight the answer.

> **ANSWER:**
> b

Click on 1 to return and discuss students' predictions.
Close the flipchart by clicking X in the toolbar.
Return to the double spread by clicking on the zoomed-up area to make it smaller.

Flipchart: *Reading* **p76**
Open the flipchart.
3 This exercise is on two pages 1 and 2 . Students work in pairs to correct the sentences in their books, referring back to the text where necessary. Click on 🖊 and ask a student to come to the interactive whiteboard and erase any incorrect parts of the sentence. Then, click on 🖊 and write in the correction above the sentence.

> **TIP:** *If students make a mistake, click on ↺ to delete the last stroke. You can change the width of the eraser by using the slider in the toolbar when 🧹 is selected.*

You can either check each page as you finish or click on 2 , finish the exercise and then click on 1 to return and check all together at the end.
Click on ☐ to display the answers in boxes below the sentences.

> **SUGGESTED ANSWERS:**
> 1 The text <u>doesn't</u> recommend having lunch in front of your computer. 2 British people send more than fifty million <u>text messages</u> every day. 3 The text says you should <u>leave</u> your phone <u>at home or switch it off sometimes</u>. 4 The <u>average</u> speed of cars in London's rush hour is thirteen kilometres <u>per</u> hour. 5 Most people <u>speed up</u> when the traffic lights turn amber. 6 The text says <u>walking</u> is probably quicker than then spelling mistake in answers flipchart (and T bk) <u>driving</u>. 7 The text suggests relaxing <u>in a garden or park</u> for twenty minutes each day.

Ask the students if there are any words in the text that they haven't understood and encourage other students to explain those words before doing so yourself. Avoid explaining the underlined words yet, as this is included in Ex. 8.
Close the flipchart.
Return to the double spread by clicking on the zoomed-up area to make it smaller.

Flipchart: *Special flipchart* **p76**
Open the flipchart by clicking on the circled area and then on the Special Flipchart button.
This area is for consolidation following the article on the 'Slow Movement'. Use the columns to make notes on students' suggestions using the pen tool 🖊. Remember, you can print out any annotations on the whiteboard.
Close the flipchart by clicking X in the toolbar.
Return to the double spread by clicking on the zoomed-up area to make it smaller.

Flipchart: *Grammar* **p77**
Open the flipchart.
6 Students complete the sentences in pairs in their books. Click on 🖊 and ask a student to come to the interactive whiteboard and write the correct form of the verb in Present Simple Passive on the lines to complete the sentences. Ask them to tick the verb in the box to show that they have used it.
Click on ☐ to display the answers below the lines.

> **ANSWERS:**
> 1 Pizzas <u>are delivered</u> in twenty minutes or you get your money back. 2 Service <u>is included</u> in the bill. 3 Many people <u>are caught</u> by speed cameras. 4 London Underground <u>is used</u> by thousands of people every day. 5 Millions of people <u>are employed</u> in the fast-food industry. 6 Customers <u>are charged</u> 35 yen per minute to eat in the Totenko restaurant in Tokyo.

> **TIP:** *Click on 🖊 to highlight irregular verbs and pronunciation of 'ed' endings.*

Close the flipchart.

Flipchart: *Vocabulary* **p77**

Open the flipchart.

10a Students work in pairs to choose the correct alternative in their books, and discuss reasons for their choice.

b Click on 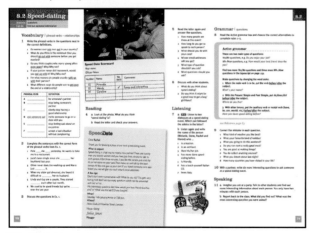 to play recording 8.3 and students listen to check their answers.

Click on ✏ and ask a student to come to the interactive whiteboard and erase the incorrect choices.

> **TIP:** *If students make a mistake, click on ↺ to erase the last stroke.*

You can either check each sentence as you work through by clicking on [answer] at the end of the sentence or check all the sentences together at the end by clicking on [answer] at the bottom. Clicking on [answer] will highlight the answers.

> **ANSWERS:**
> 1 going up 2 got worse 3 risen 4 fallen 5 deteriorating 6 gone down

> **TIP:** *After students have studied the correct answers and tried to remember them, return to [1]. Click on ✏ and ask a student to come to the interactive whiteboard and erase both choices for each sentence. Then click on ✏ and see if students can remember the missing verbs and write them in. Ask students to write above the sentences, and then you can click on [answer] for each sentence to show the highlighted verb in the space as before.*

Close the flipchart.
Click on ⏵⏵ to go to the next double spread.

Double Spread p78/79

and read through the definition with the whole class.
Tell the students to read the rest of the questions in pairs and write the other phrasal verbs next to the correct definitions in their books. Click on ⭝ and ask a student to come to the interactive whiteboard to drag the phrasal verbs from the box at the top onto the lines next to their meanings.

Click on [answer] to display the answers below the lines.

> **ANSWERS:**
> A go out with B split up with C grow apart D ask someone out E get over F put up with

> **TIP:** *For additional practice, click on ✏ and using a thick width, ask a student to come to the interactive whiteboard to blank out all the phrasal verbs. Ask students to try and tell you the words for each definition. Click on ✏, reduce the width, and slowly erase the blanks (use the highlighted answers) to check. Encourage students to rub out slowly to help students who have difficulty remembering.*

Close the flipchart.

Flipchart: *Grammar* **p79**

Open the flipchart.

8 Focus students on the Active grammar box on the interactive whiteboard and tell them to read through the notes and choose the best alternatives. Students check in pairs. If you have done the optional warmer, it is not necessary for them to find examples in the tapescript. Click on ✏ and ask a student to come to the interactive whiteboard and erase the incorrect alternatives in 1, 2 and 3.

Click on [answer] to highlight the answers.

> **ANSWERS:**
> 1 When the main verb is to be, put the verb <u>before</u> the subject. 2 With the Present Simple and Past Simple, put do/ does/did <u>before</u> the subject. 3 With other tenses, put the auxiliary verb or modal verb <u>before</u> the subject.

Tell students to look at Reference page 83 in their books and give them a few minutes to read through the notes. Ask: How many common question words are there? (8) Ask students to give you some examples with these questions words. Say: *How* – elicit a question e.g., How are you?

Ask: What other words can we put with the question word what? (*time*, *kind*) What other words can we put with the question word *how*? (*many*, *much*). What happens when the question word is the subject of the sentence? (The verb comes after the question word and we don't use the auxiliary).

If you feel students are not very confident with this, click on ➡ three times to move to a clean page and write another example on the interactive whiteboard, contrasting the question word as subject and as object of the question. e.g., 1 Who kissed the girl? (*who* is the subject and *girl* is the object) and 2 Who did the girl kiss? (*who* is the object and *girl* is the subject). Ask the students to identify the subject and the object in each sentence. Click on ✏ to highlight.

Click on [2].

9 This exercise is on [2] and [3]. Students work in pairs to correct the mistake in each sentence in their books, referring to the grammar reference page if necessary. Click on ✏ and ask a

Flipchart: *Vocabulary* **p78**

Open the flipchart.

1 Focus students' attention on the heading PHRASAL VERB on the interactive whiteboard and elicit/teach the meaning (verb + one or two particles e.g. adverb or preposition which changes the meaning of the verb). Try and elicit (use mime) an example of a phrasal verb e.g., *get up*. Focus students on the box, click on ⭝ and, as an example, drag *ask someone out* next to D. (This is done in their books). Refer students to the first question in their books

student to come to the interactive whiteboard, indicate where the mistake is, and write the correction above the question. You can either check each sentence as you work through by clicking on ▨▨ at the end of each line or check all the sentences together at the end by clicking on ▨▨ at the bottom.

Clicking on ▨▨ will display the answers below the sentences.

> **ANSWERS:**
> 1 What kind of weather <u>do</u> you like best? 2 What <u>is</u> your favourite kind of holiday? 3 What <u>are</u> you going to do this weekend? 4 <u>Can you</u> cook a really good meal? 5 <u>Are you</u> good at making things? 6 <u>Do you</u> collect anything unusual? 7 What <u>did</u> you dream about last night? 8 How many countries <u>have you</u> visited in your life?

> **TIP:** Click on 🖌, ask a student to come to the interactive whiteboard and, after students have studied each question, erase it. Click on ✏ and try to write it again. Ask other students for help. Click on ▨▨ at the end of the line to display the correct question below the space.

Close the flipchart.

Flipchart: *Your ideas* **p79**

Open the flipchart by clicking on the circled area and then on the Your Ideas button 🔲

After allowing students to read the letter containing the information about speed-dating ask them to get into groups and think of six interesting questions that they would like to ask at a speed-dating evening. Ask each group to share their information with the class by using the ✏ tool to write on the flipchart.

Close the flipchart by clicking X in the toolbar.

Return to the double spread by clicking on the zoomed-up area to make it smaller.

Click on ▷ to go to the next double spread.

Double Spread p80/81

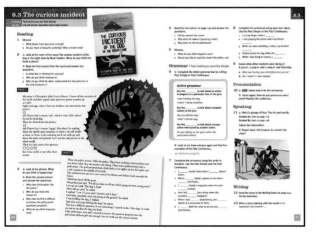

Flipchart: *Your ideas* **p80**

Open the flipchart by clicking on the circled area and then on the Your Ideas button 🔲

Use this area to collate notes on the group discussion of favourite authors and books. Perhaps you could bring in a selection of your favourite books to get discussion moving. Make notes with the pen tool ✏.

Close the flipchart by clicking X in the toolbar.
Return to the double spread by clicking on the zoomed-up area to make it smaller.

Flipchart: *Grammar* **p81**

Open the flipchart.

7 Students complete the sentences in their books in pairs. Click on ✏ and ask a student to come to the interactive whiteboard to write the correct form of the verbs on the lines provided.

Click on ▨▨ to display the answers below the lines.

> **ANSWERS:**
> 1 was walking/met 2 took/wasn't looking 3 was reading/arrived 4 were you driving/happened 5 saw/was working 6 told/wasn't listening

Click on 2.

8 In their books, students finish the sentences appropriately using their own ideas. Go around the class monitoring students' work and making any corrections. Click on ✏ and ask for volunteers to come to the interactive whiteboard to write their examples to complete each beginning. Ask students read out their sentences for the class.

Close the flipchart.

Click on the upwards pointing arrow ▨ to return to Unit 8, and then again to return to the contents page to go to the next module.

Click **page 85**. It will expand to fill the screen. Remember, you can zoom in to any part of the page by clicking on it, and return by clicking on it again.

Page 85

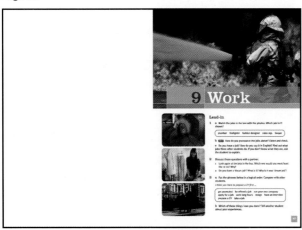

Flipchart: *Lead-in* **p85**

Open the flipchart by clicking on the circled area and then on the flipchart button AV.

3a Read through the phrases in the box on the interactive whiteboard with the class. In pairs, students put the phrases in a logical order in their books. Tell them there is not necessarily one correct answer, and that they must justify the order that they choose.

Click on ⬉ and ask a student to come to the interactive whiteboard and drag the phrases up and down until they are in a logical order.

See if the rest of the class agree or disagree with the order. Discuss and possibly amend the order. Have students give reasons for what they say.

Click on ⬚ to display the suggested answers on the right and discuss any differences.

> **SUGGESTED ANSWERS:**
> prepare a CV, apply for a job, have an interview, be offered a job, take a job, get promoted, work long hours, resign, run your own company.
> b Students discuss their experiences in pairs, using the list on the interactive whiteboard for reference. Get feedback from the whole class.

> **TIP:** *Click on* ➡ *for a blank page, click on* ✎ *and ask students to try and generate the list again and write it up.*

Close the flipchart by clicking X in the toolbar.
Return to the double spread by clicking on the zoomed-up area to make it smaller.
Click on ▷ to go to the next double spread.

Double Spread p86/87

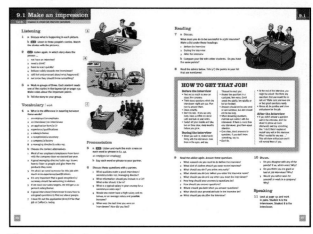

Flipchart: *Listening* **p86**

Focus students on the pictures on the interactive whiteboard. Tell them to discuss with a partner what is happening in each one.

Click on ✎ and ask a student to come to the interactive whiteboard to write suggestions along the lines provided. Discuss students' ideas.

Click on ⬚ and play recording 9.2. Students listen to the stories and match them to the pictures.

Click on ✎ and ask a student to come to the interactive whiteboard to write the conversation numbers next to the appropriate pictures. Change the pen colour and write any corrections to students ideas about the pictures.

Click on ⬚ to display the answers below the last lines and next to the boxes. There are separate ⬚ buttons if you prefer to check each task individually.

> **ANSWERS:**
> A 3 The interviewer is throwing an ashtray at the interviewee.
> B 2 The interviewee is parking in the Managing Director's personal parking space.
> C 1 An interviewee is spilling water (because he is very nervous).

Close the flipchart.

Flipchart: *Vocabulary* **p86**

Open the flipchart.

4b This exercise is on 1 and 2 . In their books, students choose the correct alternative in pairs. Click on 🍂 and ask a student to come to the interactive whiteboard and erase the incorrect alternative. You can either check each page as you finish or click on 2 , finish the exercise and then click on 1 to return and check all together at the end. Alternatively, you can click on ⬚ at the end of each line and check each sentence as you go through.

Clicking on ⬚ will highlight the answers.

ANSWERS:
1 employees 2 sales rep. 3 experience (point out to the students that experience is the correct answer because it is uncountable) 4 receptionist 5 bonus 6 interviewer 7 application form

TIP: *After students have studied the correct answers and tried to remember them, return to* 1 *. Click on* 🖌 *, increase the width and ask a student to come to the interactive whiteboard and erase both choices for each sentence in turn. Then click on* ✏ *and see if students can remember the missing vocabulary and write it above the space. Click on* ☑ *for each sentence to show the highlighted word in the space as before.*

Close the flipchart.

Flipchart: *Special flipchart* **p87**
Open the flipchart by clicking on the circled area and then on the Special Flipchart button 📝
Put the class into A groups, B groups and C groups. Group A should look at 'The International School of English' advertisement; Group B should look at 'Horizon Children's Summer School' and Group C should look at the 'Wessex University Department of Languages' advertisement.
Ask them to think about what skills you would need for each job. Then ask them to come to the board and make notes on their discussions, using the ✏.
Switch groups when A, B and C have all taken their turns.
Close the flipchart by clicking X in the toolbar.
Return to the double spread by clicking on the zoomed-up area to make it smaller.

Flipchart: *Reading* **p87**
Open the flipchart.
9 This exercise is on 1 and 2 . Read through the questions on the interactive whiteboard with the whole class. Tell students to read the text again and answer the questions in their books with a partner.
Click on ✏ and ask a student to come to the interactive whiteboard to write the answers along the lines provided. You can either check each page as you finish or click on 2 , finish the exercise and then click on 1 to return and check all together at the end. Alternatively, you can click on ☑ at the end of each line and check each answer as you go through. Clicking on ☑ will display the answers below the lines.

ANSWERS:
1 You need to find out about the company. 2 You should wear smart clothes. 3 You should go and have a coffee in a local cafe?. 4 You should take two or three slow, deep breaths. 5 You should shake hands firmly, look the interviewer in the eye and say 'Pleased to meet you'.
6 not too short and not too long 7 You should give clear, direct answers. 8 You should look at the interviewer.
9 You should be positive and show enthusiasm. 10 If you think you haven't answered a question well, you should phone the interviewer and explain yourself.

Close the flipchart.
Click on ⬚ to go to the next double spread.

Double Spread p88/89

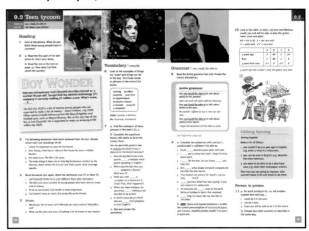

Flipchart: *Your ideas* **p88**
Open the flipchart by clicking on the circled area and then on the Your Ideas button 📝
After reading the information on young millionaires, split the class into A and B pairs. Between them, they need to discuss the pros and cons of being young and being rich. Use the columns to make notes using the ✏ tool.
Close the flipchart by clicking X in the toolbar.
Return to the double spread by clicking on the zoomed-up area to make it smaller.

Flipchart: *Vocabulary* **p88**
Open the flipchart.
Focus students' attention on the words in the box on the interactive whiteboard and ask students, in pairs, to decide which combinations with *make* or *do* are correct. Click on ⬚ and ask a student to come to the interactive whiteboard and drag the words from the box at the top into the correct column.
Click on ☑ to display the answers on the left and right of the lists.

ANSWERS:
make: an effort; progress; an appointment; a mistake; a complaint
do: nothing; your best; someone a favour

Click on ✏ and write in the examples from the book (make: money, a decision. do: business, homework.) Ask students if they can add any more.

TIP: *Click on* ✏ *and use two different colours to highlight the two groups to try and make this more memorable for the students.*

Close the flipchart.

Flipchart: *Grammar* **p89**
Open the flipchart.
8 Focus students' attention on the Active grammar box on the interactive whiteboard. Tell them to read through the notes and choose the correct alternative in their books. Students check in pairs.
Click on 🖌 and ask a student to come to the interactive whiteboard and erase the incorrect alternative.
Click on ☑ to highlight the answers.

ANSWERS:
Use <u>can</u> to talk about ability in the present. Use <u>could</u> to talk about ability in the past. Use <u>be able to</u> to talk about ability in the future.

Tell students to look at Reference page 93. Give them a few minutes to read through the notes and ask: When do we use can, could and be able to? (to talk about ability and possibility). What verb form do we use after these expressions? (the infinitive; point out that this infinitive is without *to*). Do we use an auxiliary verb? (no; point out the change of subject-verb order in interrogatives and the use of not in negatives). Click on ✏ to highlight these points in the examples on the flipchart.
Click on 2 .
9a This exercise is on 2 and 3 .
Students complete the sentences in their books and check in pairs. Click on ✏ and ask a student to come to the interactive whiteboard write the correct modal verb in the gaps.
You can either check each sentence as you finish it by clicking on ✔CHECK at the end of the line or all together for that page by clicking on ✔CHECK at the bottom. Similarly, you can check each page as you finish or click on 3 , finish the exercise and then click on 2 to return and check all together at the end.
Clicking on ✔CHECK will display the answers below the lines.

ANSWERS:
1 can 2 couldn't 3 can't/Can 4 could 5 couldn't 6 Could 7 won't be able to 8 Will you be able to

b On 3 , click on ▶ to play recording 9.4, pausing after every sentence so that the students can repeat. Point out that can is pronounced in two different ways. Elicit/model the two different ways.

> **TIP:** *Keep the audio window open and click on* 2 *or* 3 *if you want the students to be able to read the sentences as they listen and repeat.*

Close the flipchart.
Click on ▷ to go to the next double spread.

Double Spread p90/91

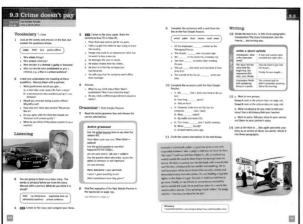

Flipchart: *Vocabulary* **p90**
Open the flipchart.
1 In pairs, students answer the questions in their books using one of the words from the box. Click on 🔖 and ask a student to come to the interactive whiteboard and drag the words from the box onto the lines next to the appropriate question.
Click on ✔CHECK to display the answers at the end of the line.

ANSWERS:
1 thief 2 police officer 3 jury 4 judge

> **TIP:** *For additional practice, click on* ↺ *to remove the answer boxes, click on* ✏ *, drag the slider in the toolbar to increase the pen width, and blank out all the new vocabulary. Ask students to see if they can remember the words (check spelling too). Click on* 🔖 *and drag the pen stroke away to reveal the words. (You could use* ✎ *to erase if you prefer.)*

Close the flipchart

Flipchart: *Grammar* **p91**
Open the flipchart.
11 Focus students on the picture in their books and ask them to describe it with a partner and to say what they think is happening. Get feedback from the class. Tell students to read through the whole text in order to get the general idea of the story. At this stage they do not choose alternatives. Then ask if there is any vocabulary they don't understand. Encourage other students to explain before intervening yourself. Students read through the text again choosing the correct alternatives. Click on ✎ and ask a student to come to the interactive whiteboard and erase the incorrect alternative.
Click on ✔CHECK to highlight the answers.

ANSWERS:
1 was given 2 felt 3 was told 4 waited 5 ran 6 took 7 told 8 was arrested 9 was taken

> **TIP:** *Click on* ✎ *and erase both alternatives. See if students can remember the right verb and form. Put the class into two teams and have a competition. Click on* ✏ *and use a different colour for each team.*

Close the flipchart.

Flipchart: *Your ideas* **p91**
Open the flipchart by clicking on the circled area and then on the Your Ideas button 🄰
Use this area to collate ideas on the topic 'crime and punishment.'
Use the pen tool ✏ to make notes.
Close the flipchart by clicking on X in the toolbar.
Return to the double spread by clicking on the zoomed-up area to make it smaller.
Click on the upwards pointing arrow 🔼 to return to Unit 9, and then ▦ to return to the contents page to go to the next module.

Unit 10

Click **page 95**. It will expand to fill the screen. Remember, you can zoom in to any part of the page by clicking on it, and return by clicking on it again.

Page 95

Flipchart: *Lead-in* **p95**

Open the flipchart by clicking on the circled area and then on the flipchart button AV.

1b In pairs, students divide the animals into four groups in their books. Tell students that some words can go into more than one group.

Click on ⟨cursor⟩ and ask a student to come to the interactive whiteboard to drag the words from the box at the top into the correct column.

Click on ⟨button⟩ to display the answers on a new page.

Click on ⟨button⟩ to return to ⟨1⟩ to compare your answers.

> **SUGGESTED ANSWERS:**
> WILD ANIMALS: tiger, lion, elephant, hyena, bear, wolf, snake, zebra, eagle, whale; DOMESTIC ANIMALS: dog, cat, horse, cow; INSECTS: spider; SEA ANIMALS: snake, whale.

c In pairs, students add two more examples to each list in their books. Click on ⟨pen⟩ and ask a student to come to the interactive whiteboard and write the names of the extra animals in the correct columns.

> **TIP:** *Click on* ⟨pen⟩*, elicit the stress for the animal words and place a 'blob' above the stressed syllable.*

Close the flipchart by clicking X in the toolbar.
Return to the double spread by clicking on the zoomed-up area to make it smaller.

Flipchart: *Your ideas* **p95**

Open the flipchart by clicking on the circled area and then on the Your Ideas button AV.

Use this area to collate ideas about favourite animals and the experiences students may have had with them. Use the pen tool ⟨pen⟩ to make notes.
Close the flipchart by clicking X in the toolbar.

Return to the double spread by clicking on the zoomed-up area to make it smaller.
Click on ⟨button⟩ to go to the next double spread.

Double Spread p96/97

Flipchart: *Vocabulary* **p97**

Open the flipchart.

7a Students complete the questions in pairs in their books. Tell them to pay close attention to the question form of the verb.

b Click on ⟨button⟩ to play recording 10.1 and students listen to check their answers.

Click on ⟨pen⟩ and ask a student to come to the interactive whiteboard and write on the lines provided to complete the questions.

Click on ⟨button⟩ to display the answers below the lines.

> **ANSWERS:**
> 1 Where <u>did you grow up</u>? 2 Who <u>brought you up</u>? 3 As a child, who <u>looked after you</u> when you were ill? 4 As a child, who <u>did you look up to</u>? 5 Have <u>you ever picked up</u> any English from TV or songs? 6 Have <u>you ever come across</u> any money in the street?

Close the flipchart.

Flipchart: *Listening and speaking* **p97**

Open the flipchart.

9a Click on ⟨button⟩ to play recording 10.2. Students listen to the woman and decide which two people most influenced her in her childhood. Students check in pairs.

Click on ⟨pen⟩ and ask a student to come to the interactive whiteboard to write the two people along the lines provided.

Click on ⟨button⟩ at the end of the question to display the answers below the lines.

> **ANSWERS:**
> Mother / Grandmother

b Read through the statements on the interactive whiteboard with the whole class and click on ⟨button⟩ to play recording 10.2 again. Students decide which statement is false and check with a partner. Click on ⟨pen⟩ and ask a student to come to the interactive whiteboard and highlight the incorrect statement.
Click on ⟨button⟩ to highlight the answer.

ANSWER:
number 4 is false as she says that she didn't take to her teachers and school wasn't easy.

If you feel students can cope with more vocabulary, explain the meaning of *take to* (like) and tell students to add it to the list of phrasal verbs in Ex. 5. You could also tell them to write an example sentence with this phrasal verb.

Click on [2].

c Focus students on the How to ... box and read through the notes on the interactive whiteboard. Click on 🔊 to play recording 10.2 again and students count the times they hear each phrase and note it in their books. Students check in pairs.

Click on ✏ and ask a student to come to the interactive whiteboard and write the number in the box next to each phrase. Click on ▢ to display the answers next to each box.

ANSWERS:
I mean ... (2); Well, ... (1); So, anyway ... (1); You see ... (1)

Explain to the students that these phrases are very common in normal conversation and help the flow and fluency of what is being said.

Close the flipchart.

Click on ▢ to go to the next double spread.

Double Spread p98/99

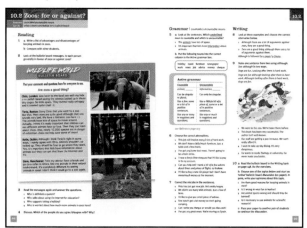

Flipchart: *Your ideas* **p98**

Open the flipchart by clicking on the circled area and then on the Your Ideas button 🖼

Put the class into A and B pairs. Ask them to discuss their opinions on putting animals into zoos. Ask student A to think about the pros and student B to think about the cons.

Make notes on the interactive whiteboard, using the pen tool ✏

Close the flipchart by clicking X in the toolbar.

Return to the double spread by clicking on the zoomed-up area to make it smaller.

Flipchart: *Grammar* **p99**

Open the flipchart.

5a Students read the sentences and answer the question in their books with a partner. Check with the whole class. Click on ✏ and write 'C' over *animals*, choose a different colour and write 'U' over *information*. Click on ▢ at the end of the sentences to display the answers at the end of the sentences.

ANSWERS:
animals is countable and *information* is uncountable

b Focus students on the words in the box and the Active grammar notes. Click on ✏ and add *animal* and *information* to the two columns. Students work in pairs to put the words into the correct column in their books. Click on ▢ and ask a student to come to the interactive whiteboard and drag the words from the box into the correct columns.

Click on ▢ to display the answers in boxes on the right and left of the columns.

ANSWERS:
Countable: holiday, newspaper, job, cheque
Uncountable: travel, furniture, work, news, advice, money

TIP: *Click on* ✏ *and highlight the two groups in different colours (choose the same colour combination as before).*

Click on ◀ to return to [1] without answers, click on ✏ and draw a third column on the interactive whiteboard with the heading **Both**. Explain that some words can be either countable or uncountable. Write *coffee*, *glass* and *hair* on the interactive whiteboard. Give two example sentences with *hair* to demonstrate the difference e.g., There's a hair in my soup; She's got red hair. In pairs, students try to write two example sentences which demonstrate the distinction for glass and coffee. Get feedback from the whole glass.

Refer the students to Reference page 103 and read through the list of uncountable nouns with the whole class. Give students time to read through the rest of the grammar rules and then ask the following questions: Do we use *a/an* with countable or uncountable nouns? (countable) Do we use much with countable or uncountable nouns? (uncountable) Do we use *a bit of* with countable or uncountable nouns? (uncountable) What do we usually use in affirmative clauses? (some) What do we usually use in negative and interrogative clauses? (any) When can we use some in questions? (when we expect the person to say yes).

Close the flipchart.

Flipchart: *Grammar* **p99**

Open the flipchart.

7 Students work in pairs to correct the mistakes in the sentences in their books.

Click on ✏ and ask a student to come to the interactive whiteboard and indicate where the mistake is. Write in any correction needed. If there is an extra incorrect word, click on 🧽 and erase it.

Click on ▢ to display the answers below the lines.

ANSWERS:
1 Pete has just got <u>a</u> new job. 2 Just a few lions. 3 I'd like to give you <u>a</u> small piece of advice 4 She hasn't got a lot <u>of</u> money ... 5 Can I write you <u>a</u> cheque ... 6 I've got <u>some</u> great news ...

Close the flipchart.

Click on ▢ to go to the next double spread.

Double Spread p100/101

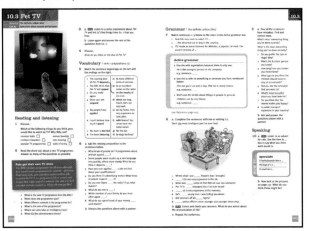

Flipchart: *Vocabulary* **p100**

Open the flipchart.

5 In pairs, students match the beginnings and endings of the sentences in their books. Click on ⬚ and ask a student to come to the interactive whiteboard and drag the endings on the right up and down until they match the beginnings.

> **TIP:** *'Park' temporarily unwanted sentence endings on top of the lines to avoid overwriting.*

Click on ▭ to display the answers on the right.

> **ANSWERS:**
> 1 c 2 a 3 f 4 h 5 g 6 e 7 d 8 b

> **TIP:** *Click on ✏ and highlight verbs and corresponding prepositions. Explain to the students that these verbs need these dependent prepositions to connect them to the object. Point out that the prepositions do not change the meaning of the verb as happens with phrasal verbs.*

> **TIP:** *Use the cover sheet to hide the prepositions. Click on ▭ in the toolbar and drag the pointer in the left quarter to the right to show the sentence beginnings with the verbs. See if students can remember the corresponding prepositions and then click on ▭ to remove the cover and check.*

Close the flipchart.

Flipchart: *Grammar* **p101**

Open the flipchart.

8a This exercise is on ① and ② . Students complete the sentences in pairs in their books.

b Click on ② and click on 🔊 to play recording 10.4. Students listen and check their answers, and then check with a partner. Click on ① , click on ✏ and ask a student to come to the interactive whiteboard to write in the missing word if necessary. You can either check each page as you finish or click on ② , finish the exercise and then click on ① to return and check all together at the end.

Clicking on ▭ will display the answers below the lines.

> **ANSWERS:**
> 1 the 2 (–) 3 the 4 the 5 (–) 6 the 7 the 8 (–)

Ask the students what they notice about the pronunciation of *the*. Click on ✏ and write students' suggestions.
Click on ▭ to display the answer below the line.
c Click on 🔊 to play recording 10.4 again, pausing at the end of each sentence while students repeat. Then tell them to practise saying the sentences in pairs.

> **TIP:** *Just click on the slider in the audio window and hold it for a few seconds to give students time to repeat and then release. This is quicker than using Pause. Also, if you want to repeat any sentences, just drag the slider back and then release. While the audio is playing, you can click on ① or ② to move between pages.*

Close the flipchart.

Flipchart: *Special flipchart* **p101**

Open the flipchart by clicking on the circled area and then on the Special Flipchart button 🅰.

This page contains five pictures of unidentified objects, covered with an erasable area. Ask a student to come out to the board and use the 🖊 tool to rub out one of the circles. He or she then has to try and describe what they think they can see. To check if he/she is right, click on the ▭ button and reveal the answer underneath. Repeat with the other circles.

Close the flipchart by clicking on X in the toolbar.

Return to the double spread by clicking on the zoomed-up area to make it smaller.

Click on the upwards pointing arrow 🔼 to return to Unit 10, and then 🔳 to return to the contents page to go to the next module.

Click **page 105**. It will expand to fill the screen. Remember, you can zoom in to any part of the page by clicking on it, and return by clicking on it again.

Page 105

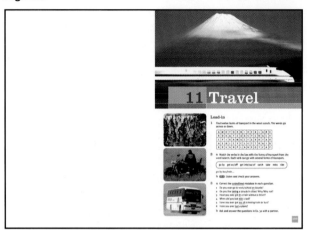

Flipchart: *Lead-in* **p105**

Open the flipchart by clicking on the circled area and then on the flipchart button AV .

1 Students work in pairs to find the words in the word search in their books. Check they understand the meaning of *across* and *down*.

Click on ✏ and ask a student to come to the interactive whiteboard and highlight the transport words they have found.

Click on ☑CHECK to display the answers on a new page.

Click on ◀ to return to 1 to compare your answers.

> **ANSWERS:**
> across: motorbike, coach, ferry, bicycle, train, van, plane
> down: car, moped, taxi, bus, lorry

Ask individual students to pronounce the words. Point out the difference between a *motorbike* and a *moped* (a moped is small and has a low-powered engine whereas a motorbike is bigger and has a high-powered engine) and *coach* and *bus* (coach is normally between cities and bus within a city). Click on ✏ and put a 'blob' above stressed syllables.

Close the flipchart by clicking X in the toolbar.

Return to the double spread by clicking on the zoomed-up area to make it smaller.

Flipchart: *Your ideas* **p105**

Open the flipchart by clicking on the circled area and then on the Your Ideas button 📝

Give students 5 minutes to write down (in groups) as many forms of transport as they can think of. Move around the class, taking one idea from each group and write it on the flipchart using the ✏ tool. Keep moving from group to group until there are no more ideas. Give points for each answer if you would like. Then discuss how good/bad each type is for the environment.

Close the flipchart by clicking X in the toolbar.

Return to the double spread by clicking on the zoomed-up area to make it smaller.

Click on ▷▷ to go to the next double spread.

Double Spread p106/107

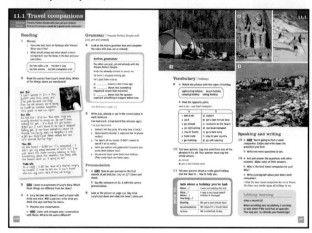

Flipchart: *Grammar* **p106**

Open the flipchart.

Students write *just, already* or *yet* in the correct place in the sentences in their books. Students check in pairs. Click on ✏ and ask a student to come to the interactive whiteboard and write the amended sentence on the lines provided.

> **TIP:** *If students would prefer to type their examples, click on* T *in the toolbar to open the text tool, click where they want to type, go to the keyboard and type. You can select different fonts, change the size, colour and background etc. If, when you close the text box, the text is in the wrong place, click on* ⬉ *and you can drag it to the correct position.*

You can either check each sentence as you finish it by clicking on ☑CHECK at the end of the line or all together at the end by clicking on ☑CHECK at the bottom.

Clicking on ☑CHECK will display the answers below the lines.

> **ANSWERS:**
> 1 Simon's already left the party. 2 Diana hasn't phoned yet. 3 I've already spent all my money. 4 Have you written any postcards yet? 5 My parents have just come back from holiday.

Close the flipchart.

Flipchart: *Your ideas* **p107**

Open the flipchart by clicking on the circled area and then on the Your Ideas button 📝

Ask students to look at the pictures of the four types of holidays. Use the flipchart area to collate ideas about what kind of holiday students would prefer to go on and why. Use the pen tool ✏ to make notes.

Close the flipchart by clicking X in the toolbar.

Return to the double spread by clicking on the zoomed-up area to make it smaller.

Flipchart: *Vocabulary* **p107**

Open the flipchart.

9a Focus students' attention on the photos on the interactive whiteboard. In pairs, students say what type of holiday they can see. Click on ⟨⟩ and ask a student to come to the interactive whiteboard and drag the types of holiday onto the picture it describes.

Click on ▨▨▨▨ to display the answers next to the pictures.

> **ANSWERS:**
> Pic A: camping holiday Pic B: sightseeing holiday Pic C: skiing holiday Pic D: beach holiday

Click on **2**.

b In pairs, students match the opposites in their books. Click on ⟨⟩ and ask a student to come to the interactive whiteboard and drag the phrases on the right up and down until they correspond with their opposite on the left.

Click on ▨▨▨▨ to display the answers on the right.

> **ANSWERS:**
> 1 d 2 a 3 f 4 c 5 g 6 b 7 e

> **TIP:** *Click on* ▦ *and drag the cover sheet to hide one of the columns. Tell students to take turns to ask each other "What's the opposite of ....? and then click on* ▦ *to remove the cover and check their answers.*

Close the flipchart.

Click on ▷ to go to the next double spread.

Double Spread p108/109

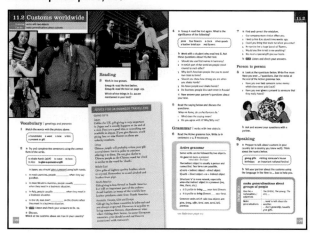

Flipchart: *Vocabulary* **p108**

Open the flipchart.

2a Students complete the sentences in their books in pairs with the correct form of the verbs in the box.

Click on ✐ and ask a student to come to the interactive whiteboard and write the correct form of the verb to complete the sentences. You can either check each sentence as you finish it by clicking on ▨▨▨ at the end of the line or all together at the end by clicking on ▨▨▨ at the bottom. Clicking on ▨▨▨ will display the answers below the lines.

> **ANSWERS:**
> 1 wave 2 shake hands 3 bow 4 kiss

Students can then discuss the customs in pairs. Then, get feedback from the whole class.

Close the flipchart.

Flipchart: *Grammar* **p109**

Open the flipchart.

7a Students correct the mistakes in their books and check in pairs.

b Click on 🔘 to play recording 11.7. Students listen and check their answers.

Click on ✐ and ask a student to come to the interactive whiteboard and write the corrections above the sentences. If there is an extra word, click on ✏ and erase it.

You can either check each sentence as you finish it by clicking on ▨▨▨ at the end of the line or all together at the end by clicking on ▨▨▨ at the bottom. Clicking on ▨▨▨ will display the answers below the lines.

> **ANSWERS:**
> 1 Our company offers you more choice. 2 I lent him 20 euros or add euro symbol about three weeks ago. 3 Could you bring me that book when you come? 4 He sent her a huge bunch of flowers. 5 Would you like to tell me anything? 6 We must give our hosts a special gift.

Close the flipchart.

Click on ▷ to go to the next double spread.

Double Spread p110/111

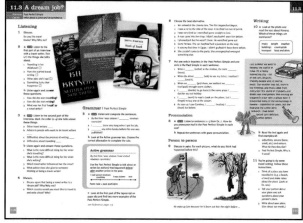

Flipchart: *Listening* **p110**

Open the flipchart.

2a Tell the students they are going to listen to an interview with a travel writer. Give them time to read through the topics on the interactive whiteboard. Check that they understand what they have to do. Click on 🔘 to play recording 11.8 and, in their books, students tick the topics they hear. Students check in pairs.

Click on ✐ and ask a student to come to the interactive whiteboard and tick those topics.

Click on ▨▨▨▨ after the topics to display the answers next to the boxes.

> **ANSWERS:**
> She talks about numbers 1, 2 and 4.

b Click on ✐ and highlight *break* in question 3. Elicit/teach the meaning of break in this context (important opportunity).

In pairs, students look at the questions on the interactive whiteboard and discuss the answers from what they remember from listening the first time to the recording. Click on ⬛ and play recording 11.8 again. Allow the students time to discuss the answers again.

Click on ✏ and ask a student to come to the interactive whiteboard and write the answers to the questions on the lines provided.

Click on ⬛ to display the answers below the lines.

> **ANSWERS:**
> 1 She started travelling with her family. 2 She wrote a diary. 3 A friend asked her to write a travel guide about Turkey.

Click on ▢2▢.
3a Read through the four points on the interactive whiteboard with the whole class and tell the students that they must put them in order in their books. Click on ⬛ to play recording 11.9. Students compare answers.
Click on ✏ and ask a student to come to the interactive whiteboard and write the numbers in the boxes to show the order. Click on ⬛ after the topics to display the answers next to the boxes.

> **ANSWERS:**
> a 3 b 4 c 2 d 1

b Allow students time to read through the questions on the interactive whiteboard with a partner and see if they remember any of the answers. Play recording 11.9. Students compare their answers in pairs.
Click on ✏ and ask a student to come to the interactive whiteboard and write the answers along the lines provided.
Click on ⬛ to display the answers on a new page.
Click on ▢ to return to ▢1▢ to compare your answers.

> **ANSWERS:**
> 1 the language 2 deciding what to include and what to leave out 3 Bill Bryson 4 Read as many travel books as you can, take a lot of notes when travelling and go for it.

Check that students understand the expression *go for it* (don't spend time worrying about what might happen, just try to do it with all your energy).
Close the flipchart.

Flipchart: *Grammar* **p111**
Open the flipchart.
7 This exercise is on ▢1▢ and ▢2▢. In pairs, students put the verbs in the correct tense in their books.
Click on ✏ and ask a student to come to the interactive whiteboard and write the correct form of the verbs in the gaps. You can either check each page as you finish or click on ▢2▢, finish the exercise and then click on ▢1▢ to return and check all together at the end.
Clicking on ⬛ will display the answers below the lines.

> **ANSWERS:**
> 1 arrived/had left 2 asked/had lost 3 got/hadn't packed
> 4 decided/had been 5 wanted/had forgotten
> 6 realised/had met

Close the flipchart.

Flipchart: *Special Flipchart* **p111**
Open the flipchart by clicking on the circled area and then on the Special Flipchart button ⬛.
This flipchart is designed to encourage creativity and to hone prediction skills. Ask students to work in small groups and use the pictures to predict what happened to each person to place them in that predicament. Put the suggestions on the board using the pen tool ✏.

Close the flipchart by clicking X in the toolbar.
Return to the double spread by clicking on the zoomed-up area to make it smaller.
Click on ▷ to go to the next double spread.

Double Spread p112/113

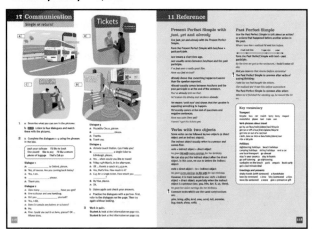

Flipchart: *Communication* **p112**
Open the flipchart.
2a This exercise is on ▢1▢, ▢2▢, ▢3▢ and ▢4▢, with one dialogue on each page. Students work in pairs to complete the dialogues in their books with the words from the box.
Click on ▢ and ask a student to come to the interactive whiteboard and drag the correct phrase from the box onto a line in the dialogue. You can either check each page as you finish or click on ▢2▢, ▢3▢ and ▢4▢, finish the exercise and then click on ▢1▢ to return and check each page at the end.
Clicking on ⬛ will display the answers at the ends of the lines.

> **ANSWERS:**
> 1: I'd like a return / That's £18.50
> 2: pieces of luggage / pack your suitcase
> 3: One pound
> 4: I'd like to book / like to pay

Close the flipchart.
Click on the upwards pointing arrow ▢ to return to Unit 11, and then ▢ to return to the contents page to go to the next module.

Click on **page 115**. It will expand to fill the screen. Remember, you can zoom in to any part of the page by clicking on it, and return by clicking on it again.

Page 115

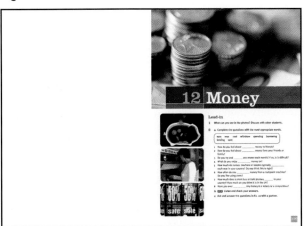

Flipchart: *Your ideas* **p115**
Open the flipchart by clicking on the circled area and then on the Your Ideas button.

Use this area to make notes on the creative ways students find to spend their new-found money! Write their ideas on the interactive whiteboard, using the pen tool.
Close the flipchart by clicking X in the toolbar.
Return to the double spread by clicking on the zoomed-up area to make it smaller.

Flipchart: *Lead-in* **p115**
Open the flipchart by clicking on the circled area and then on the flipchart button.

2a This exercise is on 1 and 2. Ask some questions to check that students understand the words in the box on the interactive whiteboard. What verb do we use with money when we talk about our jobs? (earn) And when we get money from a competition? (win) What verb do we use for the action of taking money from a cashpoint machine? (withdraw). Students complete the sentences in their books.
b Click on to play recording 12.1 and ask students to check their answers in pairs.
Click on and ask a student to come to the interactive whiteboard to drag the words from the box onto the lines in the gaps. You can either check each page as you finish or click on 2, finish the exercise and then click on 1 to return and check all together at the end
Clicking on will display the answers below the lines.

ANSWERS:
1 lending 2 borrowing 3 save 4 spending 5 earn
6 withdraw 7 cost 8 won

TIP: *Click on and highlight examples of –ing and elicit reasons.*

c Students ask and answer the questions in pairs. Get feedback from the whole class.
Close the flipchart by clicking X in the toolbar.
Return to the double spread by clicking on the zoomed-up area to make it smaller.
Click on to go to the next double spread.

Double Spread p116/117

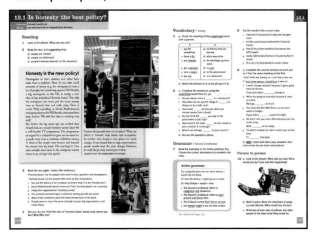

Flipchart: *Vocabulary* **p117**
Open the flipchart.
6a Click on and drag the cover up to show the questions but hide the vocabulary at the top. Tell students to look at the interactive whiteboard and try to complete the questions from memory. Allow them to look back at the table in heir books if they can't remember or to check when they have finished.
Click on to remove the cover, click on and ask a student to come to the interactive whiteboard and drag the words from the box onto the lines to complete the questions.
Click on to display the answers below the lines.

ANSWERS:
1 tip 2 cash 3 interest 4 tax 5 pension 6 salary

b Students discuss the questions with a partner. Go around the class monitoring their work and making a note of any mistakes you hear. Get feedback about the questions and then click on to go to a clean page, click on and write the mistakes you noted on the interactive whiteboard. Encourage students to correct them if they can. If not, correct them yourself.
Close the flipchart.

Flipchart: *Grammar* **p117**
Open the flipchart.
8 Students work in pairs to put the words in the right order in their books. Click on and ask a student to come to the interactive whiteboard to drag the words onto the line below in the correct order.
You can either check each sentence as you finish it by clicking on at the end of the line or all together at the end by clicking on at the bottom.
Clicking on will display the answers below the words.

ANSWERS:

1 If you had a dog, you would get more exercise. 2 He would pass his exams if he worked harder. 3 She would be much happier if she left her boyfriend. 4 If I spoke German, my job would be much easier. 5 If I had a car, I would drive to work.

Close the flipchart.

Flipchart: *Your ideas* p117

Open the flipchart by clicking on the circled area and then on the Your Ideas button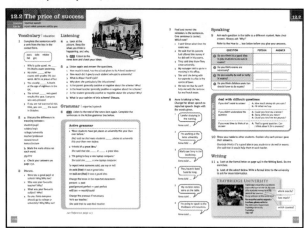

This flipchart contains a picture of a shoplifter. Use this to stimulate discussion about this issue and make notes around the picture, using the pen tool ✎.

Close the flipchart by clicking X in the toolbar.

Return to the double spread by clicking on the zoomed-up area to make it smaller.

Click on ▷▷ to go to the next double spread.

Double Spread p118/119

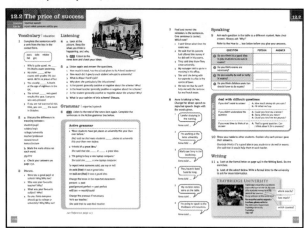

Flipchart: *Listening* p118

Open the flipchart.

4a Focus students' attention on the picture on the interactive whiteboard. Students discuss with a partner what they think is happening.

Click on ✎ and ask a student to come to the interactive whiteboard and write their ideas on the lines below the picture.

b Click on 🔊 to play recording 12.3 and tell students to listen to see if they were right. Ask students to share with a partner the things they have heard.

Click on ✎ and ask a student to come to the interactive whiteboard and write what they now think is happening.

Click on ▦▦ to display the answers below the last line.

ANSWERS:

A school is giving money to its students for getting good exam results.

Click on 2 .

5a This exercise is on 2 and 3 . Read through all the questions on the interactive whiteboard with the whole class and allow them to discuss in pairs any answers they remember from the first time they listened. Pre-teach *bribery* (when you give somebody money to make them do or not do something) and *laptop computer* (portable computer). Click on 🔊 to play recording 12.3 again

and students listen, check any answers they already have and answer the rest of the questions in pairs. Click on ✎ and ask a student to come to the interactive whiteboard and write the answers to the questions along the lines provided. You can check each page as you finish or click on 3 , finish the exercise and then click on 2 to return and check all together at the end. Click on ▦▦ to display the answers

ANSWERS:

1 £11,000 2 £500 3 head of sixth form education
4 Because it rewards everyone for doing well, not just the best students in the year.
5 She is generally negative. She says it feels a bit like bribery and students should work hard for exams because they want to do well, not for money. 6 He is generally positive because more students had got places at university than ever before. 7 She is generally positive because it made her work harder and she earned a lot of money, with which she is going to buy a laptop computer.

TIP: *For additional practice, ask students to study the questions. Click on ✎ and using a thick width, ask a student to come to the interactive whiteboard to blank out all the questions. Ask students to try and tell you the questions for each answer. Click on ↖ and drag the 'blank' away to reveal the original question.*

Close the flipchart.

Flipchart: *Grammar* p119

Open the flipchart.

8 This exercise is on 1 and 2 . Students work in pairs to report the sentences. Point out that *that* can be omitted and often is in spoken English.

Click on ✎ and ask a student to come to the interactive whiteboard and write the reported speech on the lines provided below each speech bubble. You can check each page as you finish or click on 2 , finish the exercise and then click on 1 to return and check all together at the end.

Click on ▦▦ to display the answers below the last lines.

ANSWERS:

1 Anna said (that) she preferred studying in the evenings.
2 Anna told Pete (that) she was working at the local university. 3 Anna said (that) Mark had seen Terry in the bookshop.
4 Anna told Pete (that) they hadn't lived there for long. 5 Anna said that her revision notes had been on the table.
6 Anna said she was going to speak to the Professor of Economics.

TIP: *For additional practice, ask students to study the direct speech in the bubbles. Click on ✎ and using a thick width blank out all the speech bubbles. Ask students to tell you the direct speech, click on ↖ and drag the 'blank' away to reveal if they were correct.*

Close the flipchart.
Click on ▷▷ to go to the next double spread.

Double Spread p120/121

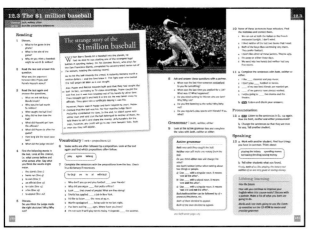

Flipchart: *Reading* **p120**

Open the flipchart.

1 Students discuss the three questions on the interactive whiteboard in pairs. Click on ✏ and ask a student to come to the interactive whiteboard and write their answers on the lines provided.

Click on 　　　 (either after each question or at the bottom) to display the answers below the last lines.

> **ANSWERS:**
> 1 baseball 2 The aim of the game is to get more runs than the opposing team. A run is scored when a batter hits the ball and then runs around the four bases before the opposing team reach a base with the ball. 3 Students' own answers.

Close the flipchart.

Flipchart: *Vocabulary* **p120**

Open the flipchart.

7 Students work with a partner to complete the sentences in their books. If you have dictionaries, allow the students to consult them where necessary. Click on ✎ and ask a student to come to the interactive whiteboard and drag the prepositions from the box at the top into the gaps to complete the sentences.

Click on 　　　 to display the answers below the lines.

> **ANSWERS:**
> 1 with 2 with 3 at 4 for 5 to 6 for 7 for 8 on

> **TIP:** *Click on ✏ to highlight verb and preposition combinations.*

> **TIP:** *For further practice, click on ↻ to remove the answers, click on ✏, drag the slider to increase the width and ask a student to come to the interactive whiteboard and blank out the last part of the sentences starting with the preposition. Then students can see if they can remember. Click on ✐ and erase slowly to give students clues if they are having difficulty remembering.*

Close the flipchart.

Flipchart: *Grammar* **p121**

Open the flipchart.

10 Students correct the mistakes in their books in pairs.

Click on ✏ and ask a student to come to the interactive whiteboard and write the correction above the sentence. Click on ✐ and erase any incorrect words.

You can either check each sentence as you finish it by clicking on 　　　 at the end of the line or all together at the end by clicking on 　　　 at the bottom.

Click on 　　　 to display the answers below the sentences.

> **ANSWERS:**
> 1 We can eat at <u>either</u> the Italian or the French restaurant tonight. I don't mind. 2 Correct. 3 <u>Neither</u> of the boys likes swimming very much. They prefer football. 4 Correct. 5 I'm away on <u>both</u> of those days. 6 Correct.

> **TIP:** *Click on ✏ and highlight the sentences that were correct.*

Close the flipchart.
Click on ▷ to go to the next double spread.

Double Spread p122/123

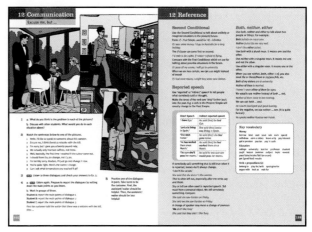

Flipchart: *Special flipchart* **p122**

Before doing any other task on the page of the Student's book, use this flipchart as an introduction to the lesson.

Open the flipchart by clicking on the circled area and then on the Special Flipchart button 🄰🌠

Due to the length of this exercise, it is on 3 pages: 1 2 and 3

Put the students into small groups and allocate them a picture each. They need to imagine a scenario and write some dialogue to act out to the class. You can then ask the groups to come out and demonstrate their 'plays', using the pen tool ✏ to write notes or key vocabulary on the flipchart.

Close the flipchart by clicking X in the toolbar.

Return to the double spread by clicking on the zoomed-up area to make it smaller.

Click on the upwards pointing arrow ⬆ to return to Unit 12, and then ▥ to return to the contents page.

Film Bank

Film Bank flipchart – London p133

Go to the Film Bank area 🎬 . Choose Unit 1. Open the flipchart by clicking on the flipchart bar.

1 Discuss the questions given on the flipchart (and make notes using the ✏ tool), using the pictures of London buildings to help the students.

Click on ② and ③ to move to the next exercise.

2 Ask students to read the questions and discuss them in pairs. Using the highlighter ✏ allow students to choose what they think is the correct answer in each case. Click on ▱▱ to see if they are correct

> **ANSWERS:**
> 1 A 2 B 3 A 4 B (5.7 million visitors per year) 5 B (built 1705) 6 B

Click on ④

Ask students to read quietly through the sentences on the interactive whiteboard. Using the pen tool ✏ , ask them to predict the correct order in which the activities happen.

Click on ▱▱ to check your answers.

> **ANSWERS:**
> Correct order: D, H, F, A, G, B, C, E

Close the flipchart by clicking X in the toolbar.

Film Bank flipchart – Summer Holiday p134

Go to the Film Bank area 🎬 Choose Unit 2. Open the flipchart by clicking on the flipchart bar.

1 Discuss the questions given on the flipchart (and make notes using the ✏ tool), using the pictures of the musicals to help the students.

Click on ② to move to the next exercise.

2 Ask students to drag the appropriate word from the box into the spaces, using the ⟲ tool.

> **ANSWERS:**
> 1 holiday 2 two 3 laughter 4 worries 5 brightly 6 blue 7 true 8 dream

Click on ▱▱ to find out the correct answers.
Close the flipchart by clicking X in the toolbar.

Film Bank flipchart – Jamie Oliver p135

Go to the Film Bank area 🎬 Choose Unit 3. Open the flipchart by clicking on the flipchart bar.

1 Look at the photos and answer the questions. Use the pen tool ✏ to write down students' ideas.

Click on ② to move to the next exercise.

2 Working in groups, ask students to put the stages into the correct order. When they have done so, ask a student to come to the interactive whiteboard and drag the steps into the right places. Use the ⟲ tool to do this.

> **ANSWERS:**
> 5 a) 8 b) 3 c) 7 d) 6 e) 1 f) 2 g) 4 h)

Close the flipchart by clicking X in the toolbar.

Film Bank flipchart – Surviving in the Sahara p136

Go to the Film Bank area 🎬 Choose Unit 4. Open the flipchart by clicking on the flipchart bar.

1 Ask students to look at the photos on the flipchart and read the information about Ray Mears. Then, using the pen tool ✏ make notes on the students' discussion.

Click on ② to move to the next page.

2 Working in pairs, students read the sentences and decide which of the alternatives is correct. When they have made their decision, ask volunteers to come to the whiteboard and erase the incorrect alternative. Check your answers by clicking on either the small ▱▱ s alongside each question, or the large ▱▱ at the bottom of the page.

> **ANSWERS:**
> 1 one-fifth 2 Sahara 3 50ºC 4 stay with 5 get in the shade 6 drink your water 7 'V' 8 scorpions

Close the flipchart by clicking X in the toolbar.

Film Bank flipchart – On Golden Pond p137

Go to the Film Bank area 🎬 Choose Unit 5. Open the flipchart by clicking on the flipchart bar.

1 Ask students to look at the photos on the flipchart. Then read the questions as a class, use the pen tool ✏ and make notes on the students' discussion.

Click on ② to move to the next page.

2 Working in pairs, students read the sentences and decide who they think will do the actions mentioned. Use the ⟲ tool to drag the appropriate letter into place.

> **ANSWERS:**
> is warm and welcoming M • kisses someone on the cheek D• is reserved and distant F • takes his/her coat off D • points at someone D• introduces someone to someone else D• shakes hands with someone B and F • walks upstairs F and B

Now watch the film and see if the guesses are correct.
Close the flipchart by clicking X in the toolbar.

Film Bank flipchart – Around the World p138

Go to the Film Bank area 🎬 Choose Unit 6. Open the flipchart by clicking on the flipchart bar.

1 Due to the length of this exercise, it is over two pages ① and ② .

Ask students to look at the pictures and read through the questions on page ① . Elicit some answers to the questions and write them in using the pen tool ✏ .

You can check the answers using the ▱▱ button now, or wait until both pages are completed.

ANSWERS:
1 English 2 Belfast and Port of Spain 3 Erie 4 Belfast
5 Port of Spain and Perth 6 Port of Spain (1.2 million)
and Perth (1.3 million) (Erie 102,000; Belfast 280,000)
7 Port of Spain and Perth 8 Erie 9 Belfast, Port of Spain
and Perth

Click on 3 to move to the next question.
2 Watch the film and ask students to fill in the blanks in their
books. When the film has finished, collate the ideas on the
flipchart, using the pen tool ✎ .
Click on ☑ to see the correct answers on a separate page.

ANSWERS:
Alison from Belfast: *18 years; the warm, friendly people;
visit the place the Titanic was built and the Albert clock;
yes*
Jennifer from Erie: *17 years; friends; - ; no*
Kathleen from Trinidad: *all childhood and teen years;-
;swimming, scuba diving, snorkelling; yes*
Astrid from Perth: *all my life until 2002; sunshine and
beaches; go to the beach; yes*

Close the flipchart by clicking X in the toolbar.

Film Bank flipchart – Carry on Doctor p139
Go to the Film Bank area ▣ Choose Unit 7. Open the flipchart by
clicking on the flipchart bar.
1 Look at the stills from the films and read the information on the
flipchart (or in the Students' Book). Ask the students to talk, in
pairs, about the questions and write some notes on the board
with the pen tool ✎ .
Click on ☑ to move on to the next page of the flipchart.
2 Tell students that the words in column A need to match the
words in column B. Ask them to work in pairs to match the correct
pairs. Then ask a volunteer to come up to the whiteboard and drag
the words (using the ▹ tool) in the right-hand column into the
appropriate places.
To check answers, click on the ☑ button at the bottom of the
page.

ANSWERS:
1 c) have an accident 2 h) go to hospital in an ambulance
3 b) do the hoovering 4 d) take a sip of tea 5 a) open the
blinds 6 e) prepare a syringe 7 f) put a thermometer
under someone's tongue 8 g) wash someone's face

Close the flipchart by clicking X in the toolbar.

Film Bank flipchart – Speed-dating p140
Go to the Film Bank area ▣ Choose Unit 8. Open the flipchart by
clicking on the flipchart bar.
1 Look at the different types of TV programme depicted in the
pictures on the flipchart (or in the Students' Book). Ask the
students to discuss the questions in small groups and write some
notes on the board with the pen tool ✎ .
Click on ☑ to move on to the next page of the flipchart.
2 Students need to put the words from the box into the correct
spaces in the sentences. Ask them to work in their books to find
the matching answers. Then ask students to come out to the
board and drag the words into place, using the ▹ tool.

To check answers, click on the ☑ button at the bottom of the
page.

ANSWERS:
1 slots 2 humour 3 addresses 4 earth 5 conversation
6 background 7 other

Close the flipchart by clicking X in the toolbar.

Film Bank flipchart – The Interview p141
Go to the Film Bank area ▣ Choose Unit 9. Open the flipchart by
clicking on the flipchart bar.
1 Ask students to read through the questions and try to answer
them in groups. Make notes with the ✎ tool.
Click on ☑ to move to the next page.
2 In groups, ask students to use the suggestions on the flipchart
to design their own training video. Each group should then come
out to the interactive whiteboard and talk through their video,
using the ✎ tool to highlight which points they have used.

Close the flipchart by clicking X in the toolbar.

Film Bank flipchart – Wolves
Go to the Film Bank area ▣ Choose Unit 10. Open the flipchart
by clicking on the flipchart bar.
1 Ask students to read through the questions and try to answer
them in groups. Make notes with the ✎ tool.
Click on ☑ to move to the next page.
2 Ask students to read the sentences and, in pairs, decide
whether they are true (T) or false (F). Use the pen tool to write their
ideas next to the sentences. Check the answers given by clicking
on the ☑ button.

ANSWERS:
1 T 2 T 3 F This was true in the past but now wolves are
found only in the most northern areas. 4 T 5 F They tend
to move in groups. 6 T 7 T

Close the flipchart by clicking X in the toolbar.

Film Bank flipchart – Gill's wild world
Go to the Film Bank area ▣ Choose Unit 11. Open the flipchart
by clicking on the flipchart bar.
1 Ask students to read through the questions on the flipchart and
try to answer them in pairs. Remember, you can make notes with
the pen tool ✎ and print out your annotations.
Click on ☑ and 3 to move to the next exercise.
2 Ask students to read the text about Gill's life. The words in the
box can be dragged with the ▹ tool and need to be matched into
the correct spaces. Ask volunteers to come to the whiteboard and
fill in the gaps. As a class, go through the answers by clicking on
the ☑ button.

ANSWERS:
1 travelling 2 writing about them 3 film crews 4 at my
desk 5 scripts 6 laptop computers 7 travel editor 8 two
million readers

Close the flipchart by clicking X in the toolbar.

Film Bank flipchart – The Ladykillers

Go to the Film Bank area ▣ Choose Unit 12. Open the flipchart by clicking on the flipchart bar.

2 Ask students to look at the photos from the film you can see on page ▣ of the flipchart and try to answer the questions in pairs. Click on ▣ to move on to the next exercise.

3 After watching the film, try to answer the questions as a class, using the pen tool ✎ to write in the correct answers.

> **ANSWERS:**
> 1 A group of musicians 2 Robbers 3 The cello case comes open and some of the stolen money falls out 4 To do something about Mrs Wilberforce

Close the flipchart by clicking X in the toolbar.

NB: All of the films in the film bank can be watched before, during or after the activities. Check the activity content and choose the best timing for your students.

Pearson Education Limited
Edinburgh Gate
Harlow
Essex, CM20 2JE
England
and Associated Companies throughout the world

www.longman.com

The right of Sharon Whittaker to be identified as author of this work has
been asserted by them in accordance with the Copyright, Designs and Patents Act 1988.

Activstudio was created and is licenced by Promethean. The publishers would like to thank Promethean and Activlingua for their invaluable help.

First published 2007

ISBN: 978-1-4058-9191-2

Printed in the UK by Ashford Colour Press Ltd

Set in Meta LF, 8.5pt

Publishing Management and Design by Starfish Design Editorial and Project Management Ltd.
Introduction adapted from material supplied by Sarah Walker.

All page reproduction material is taken from *Total English Pre Intermediate Students' Book*.
Written by Richard Acklam and Araminta Crace.
ISBN: 978-0-582-84189-5
© Pearson Education Limited 2005